In Touch with Ra

Sheila Gwillam

with a Foreword by
Paul Beard

Published by
Light Publishing

First published in 1996
by Light Publishing
The College of Psychic Studies
16 Queensberry Place
London, SW7 2EB

ISBN 0 903336 15 4 (paperback)

The aim of LIGHT PUBLISHING and THE COLLEGE OF
PSYCHIC STUDIES is to explore all aspects of spiritual and
psychic knowledge.

The views expressed in all books published by LIGHT
PUBLISHING and THE COLLEGE OF PSYCHIC STUDIES
are those of the author, and do not necessarily reflect the
views of The College of Psychic Studies.

"We have room for all who realise the importance, in a
materialistic age, of expressing a belief that there is
something behind matter and that death does not end all. . ."
*From a preliminary meeting of the College, November 1883. This
was the declared note of the then new College and it remains so to
this day.*

The cover was designed by Polly Rathbone, the colour
illustration being taken from an original painting on silk by
Sheila Gwillam.

Printed in Great Britain by
Rexham Digital Imaging Ltd, Reading, Berks.

CONTENTS

DEDICATION

I would like to dedicate this book to three souls who have travelled this far with me in this particular life; my children Brandon, Anna and Lyndon, each with their unique contribution to the enrichment of my life, with love and blessings.

ACKNOWLEDGEMENTS

When I thought about thanking people for their help in producing this book, I realised how many souls have touched my life. Many in a quiet way and others in a more direct manner. To all of you, I give my thanks.

With special thanks to The Teachers.

FOREWORD

In all communications claiming a post-mortem source, there exists a difficulty that cannot be fully overcome. This is because the words spoken or written do not have a single source; an intermediary is necessary in the form of a sensitive or medium. The result is a partial collaboration. Even if he should wish to, the post-mortem communicator cannot thrust this other element aside as if it were a physical veil. In expressing the communicator's qualities of being as best she can, something of the medium's own qualities, including her best ones, become absorbed into the result, giving it this quality of a joint production. The medium has a very valuable part to play; without her the subject matter would not come into being.

In spite of this joint factor, readers often attempt to judge the material by its degree of resemblance to the past earth self of the communicator. If, like Raynor Johnson, he was a scholar well-versed in scientific method, and also a lover of literature, a double burden falls upon the medium. A good many readers will tend to demand, as a test of its genuineness, an exact reproduction of his earthly style. They do not readily allow for the delicacy of the medium's own contribution. The particular liveliness of this book illustrates that it cannot be one hundred per cent in the style Raynor chose to adopt as a writer. Indeed we see a part of him that was largely excluded from his books, and it is easy to see how this is the case.

As Raynor indicates, when he was Master of Queen's

College, University of Melbourne, a thousand students passed through his hands each year. In this book we meet more of the Raynor whose work lay in endeavouring to touch the inner self of these lively and no doubt often somewhat materialistic youngsters. In the main corpus of his books, Raynor wrote as a scholar in precise terms, as far as his subject allowed him to do so. In the present communications we see Raynor permitting himself a certain informality, a little of the vernacular, such as he may well have used in his day-to-day lectures to students, but which he excluded, for instance, in the important group of lectures he delivered both in America and at London's College of Psychic Studies, published subsequently as *Light of all Life*. In both works, however, the underlying theme remains the same serious one: that of finding and then learning from the working with the inner self that is an essential part of every being. This is in its higher reaches the same self sought by the mystics, which having found, they then looked beyond. This search lies in the heart of those who tread as yet a humble path along the mystical road. Whilst the presentation in these talks is thus lighter and more informal, the theme is entirely serious at heart.

It is interesting that Sheila Gwillam, the medium for these talks, was herself once a pupil of Raynor. This will have prepared the road for her in what must have been an unusually difficult set of communications to absorb and transmit through her own more fluid temperament. Her task of course was to lend herself as totally as she could to what Raynor had come to say. It is natural that he showed something of the more informal self she had known when she studied with him.

Some used to Raynor's former precise and crystalline style may at first find it a little hard to accept the looser style of this book. Its full seriousness is perhaps best seen in a second reading when Raynor, in quest for the Spirit, will be found as much present as when he was speaking of the search more formally. A good deal will be found that is enjoyable as well as profitable. Raynor's characteristic modesty too is never far away. Without hiding his insight, he speaks still as an earnest student among other students.

Paul Beard

NOTE AND WARNING

Sheila Gwillam met Raynor Johnson in Australia in about 1967. She attended many of his lectures concerning the spiritual path. This was where she was introduced to meditation and yoga, both of which she has continued to practise to this day.

It was on a visit to the Spiritualist church in England that Sheila was advised to try automatic writing. Telepathic messages soon began to come into her mind and, later, spiritual teachings began to form the bulk of the writings. Sheila put much of this advice into practice, and gradually began to trust the spirit helpers, not as people who had to be obeyed, but as souls who could see just that bit further and who made wise suggestions on how to observe particular situations and what lessons could be learned.

Sheila feels that thirty years of meditation, study, writing from Spirit, as well as experience of life, was all part of the training which has enabled her to write this book, given by those Beings who have gone further into life and light, but who have the compassion to come and help those of us who are seekers on the Path. Raynor always insists that he is simply the spokesman for a group of souls in the light. Sheila likes to think that she is just another link in the chain.

The problem of trying to communicate is that the health of the sitters, and the physical, mental and emotional field of the medium, as well as the communicator's ability, all have an effect on the success or the failure of working together at a moment when a psychic bond calls, and Beings from the dimensions beyond time bring teachings to the earthly plane.

The mind of the medium can be both a help and a hindrance. Spiritual knowledge gained by the medium can help, but too many preconceived ideas can colour the teachings given and therefore pollute the purity of the communication. This fact is taken into consideration before Spirit Beings even attempt to work with a group. They do their best to help all those whose desire for knowledge is sincere and truly serious.

Dabbling from ignorance into psychic phenomena is not advised. This can bring about unhealthy conditions to those foolish enough to attempt it. Therefore, any approach should be made in the light of serious research and with, at the very least, one person who has had previous experience and teaching, and always with love and light.

INTRODUCTION

Early in 1991 when the Gulf War appeared imminent, I was invited to join a group of friends who hoped to be able to undertake rescue work for the soldiers and airmen who had died in action. We did this using clairvoyance at first. After several meetings, two members of the group were able to go into an altered state of consciousness and allow a Spirit Being to speak through the medium to other members of the group. Some would simply tell the story of their passing over into the next life but others did not seem to know that they had died.

The group would gently point out that they no longer had a physical body and that they should look around them to see if they could see a friend or a light. The group would send love to the Spirit Being and many times joy was reflected in the medium's face as the Spirit Being met someone they had loved whilst on earth or become aware of a lightening in consciousness.

Later, when the war had finally finished, we began to receive teachings from Spirit, and on 12th November 1992 a new voice with beautiful diction spoke through Sheila Gwillam. It seemed as if the communicator was a trained and knowledgeable teacher. He said that the medium had known him in Australia and that it had been agreed before incarnation that they would come together to work for Spirit. When he said, "The watcher on the hill is the higher being of the inner self", I suspected who he might be and asked if he was the author of the book *The Watcher on the Hills*. He replied, "yes", and I knew we were talking to Dr. Raynor Johnson, whose books I admired and whom Sheila had known years before in Australia.

Dr. Johnson, who passed in 1987, achieved first class degrees in both arts and science subjects. He had done scientific research on spectroscopy and written a number of excellent spiritual books. He had been a Master of Queen's College at the University of Melbourne and, as he told us later, he had had the privilege of teaching 1,000 students a year for 33 years. When I asked him if he found the spirit world different from what he had imagined, he replied, "The only thing that is unexpected is, it is more wonderful than I really thought it could possibly be."

Now we began to have regular visits from Raynor, who gave us the talks that became the content of this book. He was always friendly, humourous and encouraging; understanding the limits of our knowledge and finding simple analogies to explain complex ideas.

After an article I wrote about Raynor's return was published in 1993, I received a letter from Paul Beard, former President of The College of Psychic Studies. It said he had been waiting for the return of Raynor ever since his passing and he asked if there was a possibility of hearing recordings of the talks. I sent him copies of these, and in September 1993 Paul came down to Devon to sit in the circle. Raynor came through at once and, although he was almost overwhelmed with emotion, it was wonderful to hear these two old friends of many lives talking to each other through the entranced Sheila Gwillam. Paul is possibly the most experienced assessor of mediums one could meet. At the conclusion, he turned to Sheila and said simply, "You have achieved."

It was Paul who then arranged for the transcribing of the tape recordings which make up the present book.

All of us in the group have come to love Raynor's talks and, although we now have six mediums who are often busy with rescue work, Raynor still drops in from time to time. He is so easy and friendly it is hard to remember that he returns to realms of light so elevated that form, as we know it, has been discarded.

Michael Evans

ONE

The Structure of Time

I think you will gather who I am in a moment.

These moments in time when we are together give us a glimpse into infinity. We have difficulty from your side with the timing because we are more used, in a sense, to not having the same time structure as yourselves. We have to try to time it so that we arrive when you are available. This means tuning into your daily work schedules so that we may not interfere at other moments, and the power varies. Therefore we have to gather assistance around us so that the power will build, and, of course, we have a new person with us today.

This business of time – I think perhaps you would like to know a little more about its structure. Your soul self, of course, is beyond time. It is only whilst in the body that you live by the clock, by the sun, by the seasons. This you know. Yet how much time do we actually give to this thought: how much everything is geared by the clock? Only when you go into your inner self can you become aware of this timelessness, that you are truly a part of this infinity that stretches beyond anything that the normal man's mind can even consider. If you do not give time to quietness and to going within yourself, going beyond the personality, you will never find this timelessness. You'll never understand the nature of infinity unless you find the moment in your time to do this. To do this frequently would assist you in your life, in the unfolding of your life's pattern so that you would know why you're doing what it is you are doing. You would put more effort into developing (unfolding, perhaps, would be a better expression), unfolding your inner nature and having a sense of your true being. It is since I have come to this side that I appreciate the teachings that I was given myself, into which I was searching all my life, more deeply towards the latter part. I can only reiterate that I'm very glad that I had some very good teachers, so that I was able to impart the information to my students. Many of the books I collated from other authors' information. It was my last book that I really felt that I put my soul into, but then I did have help from a lady who was also a medium and she was able to give me a great deal of information and taught me both how to go deeper into meditation and how important it is, particularly as we get older, to seek the nature of life after death.

You would not go on a journey without gathering information as to where you were going and as to how you were getting there. Surely you would look into books and read information given to you by people who had already been there, and you would get yourself a ticket. You would not dream of going anywhere without a ticket. Your ticket is meditation, going into your inner being. Information from myself is one thing but you need to experience for yourself. It is only second-hand if it is through someone like myself, even if it is in discussion with each other. To experience it yourself you must know. That is your ticket. So instead of passing over totally confused as to what has happened to you, you can go on your journey knowing your destination is the right one, so that you will be ready and not shocked, thus having to be treated, almost like going into hospital. Those who pass over are helped but sometimes they will refuse to be helped. They close themselves off with their minds. Their minds bring the shutters down so they do not see us there when we wish to help them. It is better if you pass over with your eyes open and your mind open – your mind is like your eye, your inner eye. You only see symbols through your eyes. It is your mind that interprets what you are seeing. If you have that inner eye open when you pass over, you pass straight into the light and you can avoid having to go into a hospital-type place. These are very good, and people there are well looked after, but would it not be better to arrive with your faculties all intact? It is rather like going on holiday and having to spend most of your time in hospital. This would not be very good. All I can do from my side is encourage, in the same way that I taught my students. I encouraged them; I did not bully them. I laid the facts and information before them. They were intelligent people. You are all intelligent human beings. Use your mind to assess the facts but find the facts out first. Gather your information from all areas of life. There is so much information. You hear people say that nobody has come back to tell us. This is so ignorant and so futile, it leaves people in the dark. There are facts, there is information, there's a mass of information. Look about you. There are people willing to talk about it. There are so many who say I don't want to know. This is very sad but we do our best, do we not?

Have you found anything different from what you expected when you went over?

The only thing that is unexpected is it is more wonderful than I really thought it could possibly be. To be rid of a body that is beginning to deteriorate, to leave a mind that is becoming confused simply because the physical deteriorates, to meet up with one's relatives and friends that one loved – not the ones you don't love, who are not around on your level – but to be with beings of a like nature. To experience that inner peace which we should all be able to experience whilst on the earth plane but sadly do not. To be able to have the freedom to move wherever we want to go. To go wherever we want to go. To study in the Halls of Learning, to have many, many more books. Of course, I was in my element. I was in a library with books, rows and rows of books, infinity was not really long enough! But each to their own. To someone else that would not seem heavenly, would it?

When you are on your side do you still meditate to move forward, or is it like that all the time? I mean a sort of meditation all the time?

This is a very interesting question. If you have meditated before, whilst on the earth plane, it becomes part of your being and you can learn from teachers on our side. We do gather together in groups to meditate, to learn to go even deeper into our beings, to prepare ourselves for the higher levels.

So yes, we do. Because you're on the level to which you are drawn you think for a while that this is heavenly, this is perfect, nothing could be greater. But the teachers tell us that there are levels beyond, for which we need to prepare ourselves and we've learnt to trust these teachers and, of course, we have experienced the different levels previous to the one that we are on now. So we trust the teacher who tells us this and therefore we learn to go even deeper into our meditations to prepare ourselves and to experience a little of what there is to come.

So our meditation here is preparation really for that; it's good to do it?

That is so. It also helps you in your life on the level that you are already on, so that the energy penetrates every cell of your body. It clears away some of the blockage from this and past lives, and illuminates your whole being. It empowers your aura.

Have you come to a level where you understand how you drop the temporary personality prior to perhaps taking on another personality for another incarnation? This is a subject I'm often asked about.

Mm ..... a deep thinker here! The personality that you have is rather like an imprint. I'm trying to think of an example. Take copper. Copper is copper in whatever form you mould it but you can mould the copper into many forms and shapes. In fact you can make it look totally unlike that which it was originally in the ground and people will say it is a different substance. In a way this is rather like people's personalities. They seem to be different because they are in a different form. They are influenced by the maleness and femaleness that they have taken on in that particular incarnation. So when they pass into the other levels the negative aspects are not so dominant, depending on which level they have come to. There will be more of the Godliness demonstrated, depending again on which level of spiritual evolvement they are on.

When preparing to come back to the earth plane there are some memories of the last incarnation, or even the one that they have been choosing to use on the level they were on, so that when they come back they have something that they had before but it is in a different form and different body. The different substances of the body also influence the personality they use, in other words the copper has taken on another form, if you follow.

It's rather like when you're dying, when the old self seems to drop away. When you're a child, for instance, you are the same person as when you're older but you look different and you could even be said to be a different personality. You are not exactly the same as you were when you were a child, or so it would seem. So that when you're passing out of your old body and your old personality, that falls away because it was to do with the earth, and when you arrive into the spirit world you feel anew, but you're still you. The individuality within, the individual consciousness within, is still there, you do not lose that, whatever level you go to. That is what we are assured of.

I understand that some people who perhaps come on to another level of the spirit or esoteric world find that there is a great deal of debate on the subject of reincarnation. Some maintain it is so, some maintain it is not so. At the level you're at, is this an accepted concept?

It is accepted that we can choose.

The point is that it is a voluntary act?

This is so. We can leave it for a long time or we can go on to another dimension. On lower levels there is still a great deal to debate about, and some people are aware of their past incarnations; they know what they have been. Others do not and some perhaps know about one or two. I think you've had one or two of your visitors who have explained that they know they've had a past incarnation but they don't yet know what they were. I think you'll find this amongst people on the earth level also; some do and some don't; whereas others do not need to. They can go to another planetary system if they like.

I wondered if any of your family had already reincarnated, your grandparents or such?

My grandparents are on a different level. My grandfather is on the same level as myself. My grandmother is on a level a little lower. She will have to reincarnate again and many of the other past relatives have already incarnated, in fact some have come through as my grandchildren.

Do you know if you will reincarnate?

It's not something I would wish to do. It is too wonderful on this side and at present I do not wish to.

TWO

God Consciousness

There is the need to bring God consciousness into your daily conscious life. It is deep within your being but unfortunately the link with most people has not been made. It is only when the spirit is felt deep within that a person decides that there should be more to life than just the daily grind of going to work, of feeding, looking after the children. When this – the spirit I mean – when the spirit is felt then the soul begins to ask questions, or the personality I should say, begins to ask questions because it is the soul or the God-self which is trying to make connection with the ego-self. Of course the ego-self doesn't wish to share anything with anybody, therefore it feels threatened. But the spirit continues to move and push itself up into the conscious mind. This is when some difficulties in your life can be felt. You wish to try new things and if you are with a partner who is rather set in their ways and the spirit has not started to move with them, they think you are going a little peculiar. It helps of course if both of you have the same wishes, or if the spirit within both of you moves at the same time, but this rarely happens, unfortunately. Once the spirit starts to move within you, you will find, or you probably have found, that you come across books which just seem to open at the right page and answer the questions that you have in your mind. You meet people of a like mind, or perhaps people who know a little more than you, who can point you in the right direction, and this you've probably already experienced. You share your thoughts and ideas and the spirit continues to move within you. When the God consciousness surfaces into your conscious mind this is when you are fully illumined. Up to that point you become more and more aware of your failings, rather – you may get a flash at the beginning of this – an awareness that there is much more to life than you have experienced up to now. This is rather like being taken up to the top of the mountain by helicopter and unfortunately the helicopter comes down again and you are left with the memory. This memory is what continues to draw you on. It is your little bit of evidence in your life. It is something that is true to you but which you cannot really prove to anyone else. This is your little bit of light which will draw you on like a magnet so that in times of trouble, when there are times when you wish you could give up the spiritual path, it is this light which draws you on and on. Many times you think this is all nonsense and you would like to drop off the pathway, but it continues to pull. Unlike any other thing in your life, at a certain point in your life, it is practically impossible to give it up. You may think at times it has given you up, but this is just the ego again, doing battle. It knows it's on its last legs and that it has to fight for its life. It is almost as though it is a separate entity from you yourself at times, but this is why there seems to be so much warring or so much being at war in the personality with the spirit within. It is you trying to make a conscious decision as to which path you're going to take, the left-hand path or the right-hand path. If you have been fortunate enough to be put in touch with the teachers of a spiritual nature this can help you greatly, because you can move along together instead of feeling so totally alone, because most of us feel, probably right from early on in our lifetimes, that we are in fact on our own. Most people I have spoken to about this have said that they felt that they were on their own and that nobody else seemed to think along the same lines as they did, but at some point in their life they meet up with people who have had similar experiences. They are able to confer with one another and you realise you are not on your own and, of course, the more you come in touch with people on our side of life then you realise you're never on your own if you don't want to be. We obviously don't intrude on you if you don't want to have people around you, but we are there if you need any help. We do our best.

Obviously, this subject is a very deep one and is something that you have to study and read about, although it is never quite the same as actually living it you understand. Now is there any question that you would like to ask, particularly about this, before I go on?

I don't quite understand why we have an ego when it causes so much aggro. Here you're saying to me that I have a constant battle with the ego, but why do we end up with it in the first place?

Because the ego is really this point of 'I' which is connected with the personality; that is a person who says I am this, I am that. It is nothing you can actually point to. It's one of these rather abstract things. Why we have to have it is a very good question, but one about which we all have our individual ideas. It just comes with the territory. I do not myself have an answer for it other than it's the 'I' that we use. Our personality says 'I want a house', 'I want these clothes', 'I want this food'. It is a sort of survival in the earthly life and it should have stayed under the control of the higher self but, as we came lower down the scale of vibrations, we tended to forget about the higher consciousness and the ego took over. In fact it made itself a god and people worship themselves, in that sense, rather than in the higher sense. You understand?

I have heard suggested that at some stage, long ago, spirits found themselves incarnated in the body of the higher mammals and this has caused a problem ever since for us; in a sense, they were not originally in material bodies.

It's very difficult to try and remember back that far. We have been told that when the earth was of a higher vibration nothing was as solid as it is now, but the trouble is, when you're actually in that band of vibration, whichever band of vibration you're on, it feels fairly solid to you at the time. From what I see and from what I understand, it seems that the all pervasive spirit which is God, in my understanding, is within everything, so that whatever form was taken on the planet would still have the God energy within it, and the spirit, in some strange way, seems to go through every form possible on its stage to perfection. We cannot see the end – the perfection – in one direction any more than we can see the imperfection in the other direction, if you understand that. It's within infinity but exactly how large is infinity is somewhat of a mystery and the beginnings and the endings of each planetary system go within the boundaries of the infinite, if there are any boundaries at all. The reptilian parts seem to be in our brains. We have the part in our brain that is the reptilian brain. I surmise, that is something of a left-over from our incarnations within the beast-like bodies. This is not something that everyone would agree to, or agree with, but this is, as far as my understanding goes, that we have been through life on the planet in other forms. We do not go back. Some people do not agree with this either but once you've gone beyond the animal you do not go back, not on the earth plane. If somebody has misused their human body and used the negative forces while they've been on the earth plane, then unfortunately, on the lower astral levels, they can look rather animal-like but they never actually return to animals as such. You understand?

It is mainly a dropping away as you go through your life. You often wonder where it is, this God consciousness, and what can you do to acquire it, but you don't need to acquire it. You've already got it. It just happens to be very deep within and covered over by layers of acquired ways of thinking which you've gained through past incarnations, but you have to recognise these acquired thoughts because we tend to think that every thought we think is our own, and of our own creation, when in fact it has been acquired, possibly many, many lifetimes ago and you still haven't dropped it. But at least it comes into your conscious mind so that you can recognise it. In your negative thinking – of always perhaps thinking it's the other person's fault – you may not even realise that that's what you're doing. But if you wish to take responsibility for your own spiritual life then you have to say, 'Well, it may be partly the other person's fault but it must be partly mine because of some karmic link'. Once you start recognising this you are beginning to take responsibility for yourself. Only by taking responsibility do you have any power over your own life. Every time you pass the responsibility to somebody else there's nothing you can do about it. You can't change the other person. You can only change yourself and we know how difficult that is. Yet we expect other people to change for us all the time, yes?

So, if you can, feel sympathy for the other person, that they don't even know what they can do, that they are only being ridiculous acting in egotistical fashions. Step aside and think that is where I was yesterday; but today, thank God, I'm coming into God's consciousness – I can do something about myself, and the God within me will help me to change or let go (it's more a letting go rather than changing). We use these words but they don't always accurately describe what we're actually trying to do. In my book I have written it is rather like peeling an onion, you take off the veils one after another and you are left with the pungent essence of the onion. If you can, think of that, or something more beautiful than the smell of an onion, then this is rather like being in touch with your higher self. It is not something you can point to, it is not even something they can find when they dissect the brain, it is just your very essence. It is you in purity. The more you become in touch with your higher self the better a healer you can become also. You can channel the God powers and the more you get rid of your own blocks the clearer and purer the energy and the more you understand others.

When you recognise your ego-self you get to understand other people much better because the more of your higher self you see, and the more of your lower self you see, the more you know of humanity.

Do people reincarnate in families?

Oh, quite often, yes. Not always.

But do they also reincarnate in soul groups which are larger than families?

Yes. I was a member of a soul group, or am a member of a soul group, I should say. We knew that a certain teacher was going to be on the planet at a specific time so we, all of us who were linked with this person, were fortunate enough in getting born into these families. Fortunately we had karmic links with other people who could provide us with the physical bodies and we could be born in any part of the world, but we were magnetically drawn to our teacher whilst this person was on the planet, and who still is on the planet. Some of us meet with our teacher briefly for a short period of time. We become rather like a spaceship that goes in the direction of a planet and, as it enters the magnetic field, is held for a while before drawing away and going off in a different direction. The impetus of meeting a spiritual teacher is rather similar. He or she can give you that impetus to carry on in the specific direction that may be necessary for the unfoldment of your spiritual path. Otherwise you may just muddle along doing the best you can, but not really knowing where you have to go or even knowing whether you are on the path. We were very fortunate; we did have some assistance in this respect. Unfortunately I have not completely worked off all my karma and I may have to come back at some date, somewhere in the distant future, as I think I mentioned, but not for some time. I am able to experience more of the light here and gain inner strength if you like, and come back to speak with people like yourselves so that we don't completely lose our link with you. We actually only ever lose the link in our conscious minds.

I have been told that a new world teacher will come to lead the world into a new stage. Have you heard of this?

There always seem to be so many new world teachers about and putting in an appearance. This is something I personally don't know a great deal about. I understand more about the God energies interpenetrating everything. There are obviously going to be one or two persons who may be more awakened than most, who will look as though they're going to be world teachers, but you'll find it is only in a part of the world. There will always be other parts of the world who have never heard of them and who will not hear of them. The Christ energies and the God energies are there all the time within everything and everyone.

Unfortunately we do not know everything on this side. Our teachers on the higher levels tell us that there are Beings who draw close, not necessarily in a physical body, but who will help souls who wish to spread the word further afield.

Are you in touch with other groups like this one?

We of like mind all link up together, yes. We are in contact telepathically and we are well aware of the work that is going on, so we try to channel this energy into a web-like network of light so the energies can gradually be spread into the dark areas. I mean dark from our point of view. We try to link up with people who are of a spiritual mind, who wish to travel and perhaps carry the energies into areas that would not necessarily be easy for us to go into. That way, if we make the link they can make a link with the people who seem rather dark, who are in the dark spiritually. Sometimes, in a way that I was speaking of just now – as a spiritual teacher can help – we can sometimes help in a smaller way, or you can do that in a smaller way. You probably observe this yourselves.

Is there any way in which anybody can take on anybody else's karma?

Only very special teachers, special souls who have come with that ability to transmute someone else's karma under very special circumstances. But we always have to make allowance for the Grace of God.

THREE

Discrimination Between Values

We need to learn to discriminate between the different values that we have acquired through our lives. Now first of all you have to become aware of the type of values that you have acquired from your parents, from your teachers, and from other people that you have met during your lifetime. These values you have probably assumed as your own now, because they have become part of your being. But you are becoming aware that the values you have may need some reassessing. To learn to discriminate about that which is of continuous use for your spiritual progress, you need to learn to drop, as being unnecessary, some of the values that you have acquired. Because you've had them for such a long time you will probably feel as though you're throwing out something that you really need. It's rather like a piece of furniture. You're so used to it. It has always been there, and you might as well hang on to it until the end. Well in this way, these values are the actual structures upon which you hang your personality. Do you follow this simile at all?

They are the bare bones of your persona. The rest of the things are rather like the padding or the outer fillings on the building. The padding becomes the outward show. Therefore you have to rub away at the outward show. This is when your ego gets a little battered by somebody else's opinion, if it is not a good opinion of course. We all like good opinions and would rather do without bad ones, making somebody else's opinion more valuable than your own. Maybe this has not occurred to you. Why do you get so upset if somebody's opinion of you is not good, when your own opinion of yourself should be more valuable, yes? You're not sure deep down of your own worth because you are operating from your persona or your ego, rather than your God-self. When you are aware of your God-self you are aware of your inner value, you are aware of love, you are aware of all that is good. When you're operating through your ego you are not so sure because all the opinions acquired have been somebody else's. Mixed up, rather like a bowl of soup, throw a lot in and you get a different flavour, a different blend and you lose sight of the original ingredients. Now all these opinions are bombarded at you from television, from radio, from books and newspapers, from other people. It all goes into the soup, gets mixed up and you lose sight of the original ingredient. Right? Well by learning to try and see your own thoughts rather like this, you can then learn to drop them or discard them as no longer necessary. But through meditation you're pouring in fresh energy, the love energy, which brings all this to the surface, and for a little while you can go through what seems like hell. You are alone with yourself as you would not like to be. You become more aware of what you are not, you feel inferior to someone, and superior to someone else, both of which feelings you would rather do without. You don't want to feel inferior, you don't want to feel superior and so the battle is on. Where is the you in between? It's rather like being squashed between a rock and a hard place. Neither of them would be very comfortable. But do not despair, my friends. It is actually a sign that things are moving, that things are happening. You are actually doing what you are supposed to be doing. You are becoming aware. You are channelling the God energies. Do not give up at the last moment. There are only a few more steps to go to the next level! Then, as you come to a little more peace and a little more understanding, you are able to give out more love to people on this next level and, as you become aware of your own weaknesses, the more you are aware of other people's. Having got through that nasty bit you then become aware that you have more compassion and you have less desire to criticise because you know just what it's like. You have been there and you know the difficulties, so it makes you bite your tongue a little more and not be so ready to pass judgement. This is the learning of discrimination, this is what we really mean by spiritual discrimination.

Now if you try to put these little dissertations into practice – I know you won't remember them all, all at once – you will probably find that if you listen to your centre here *(pointing to the centre of forehead)*, the thought will come to mind at the appropriate time. Just possibly when you may need it. It's rather like a lifeline. The thought comes to you, the awareness comes to you when you may be at your lowest, just when you really need it. This is your lifeline – through meditation, this is what will help you continually. Continually, of course, it stirs up the lower, but I believe this is what you desire to do in this lifetime. I believe you are all at this particular point in life, even though you may not have all been together. Don't let this worry you. We are all linked together when we have this desire to know more and to really work at ourselves. In trying to improve ourselves we then improve our own environment which has much more effect than trying to change somebody else. Because you come to realise how difficult it is to change yourself, you cannot therefore expect anyone else to change just because you want them to. But if you really want to help them, you become aware of your lower self and your higher self, you understand? It balances out so that you become aware that you are in the middle of the seesaw so to speak. You are not running from one side to the other any more. You become more and more balanced and the energy, the God energy, is much more powerful than your own ego energies. To sit quietly in a room emanating this energy is far more effective than a great deal of talk, though of course talk is necessary for certain situations and certain times. I do not denigrate talk but learn when to talk and when to keep quiet. It is hard but so very necessary. It takes away the need to feel as though you have to say something on every subject all the time. You no longer need to be at the centre or need to feel inferior, because nobody else is taking any notice of you. I know it is difficult, I've already been there and I'm not that far ahead of anyone else either.

Do you still have a lower self to contend with or are you free of that now?

Well, it's not so much seen as a lower self from our point of view at my particular level. A lot of the sifting has been done and of course a lot of the things that happen on the earth bring it to the surface much more readily. On our levels we do not have this conflict all the time; therefore if I do have a lower self it does not intrude too frequently, you understand? Of course, if I come back to the earth plane for a life, I've no doubt it will be brought to my notice!

In fact there's a purpose of our physical life to stir that up and cleanse it?

Yes, to cleanse and to stir and to do our little bit, you know, to stimulate the desire to progress, to help where we can without actually ... it's getting the balance between interfering and helping, learning to understand what we mean by helping and not taking over someone else's karma. You may be taking away their particular lessons from them. On the other hand you cannot sit back and say 'Oh, I can't help them, they have their karma'. It may be they can't help themselves, and that you should help them, O.K? But it doesn't mean that you take away the task or their lessons. Just be there to pick them up or catch them if they fall. Don't let them land on you and squash you. If they will persist in taking a jump without a parachute after you have warned them then they must take the consequences. It's rather like that, you know. If they cannot see the dangers, and you have warned them, there's no point in your standing underneath them as they land, having forgotten the parachute! I know it is rather a silly analogy but I think it describes my meaning in a much more interesting fashion, do you not think?

Could I ask if you find that you have made progress since you have been over and in what respect?

Let me see now ..... this is the difficulty in assessing whether one has progressed. One is feeling very happy, one feels that one has already arrived. It is a little difficult to assess whether one still is progressing but of course I still go to my ...... we have classes, meetings where we come together with the Higher Beings. They do come to help us. I believe the Indians call it a sitting at the feet of the Masters and absorbing the energies (shakti); that is the way it works.

People feel the light, they feel the radiation and they feel the love more sensitively. They are more aware of the love. Those who haven't become aware of the love become more aware of their lower selves and decide that that is not the place for them or that the teacher is a terrible person. In those who have become aware that this is what happens, it will stimulate both the good and the bad. You understand? And this is very similar for us when we go to these meetings, although of course the negative aspect is not so intense. We may become a little uncomfortable with the light. That is why they only come for short periods of time because we cannot stand the power for too long. It's rather like sitting out in the sun for too long. A little bit at a time is very healthy but we don't want to be burnt to a cinder. It's a little difficult because it goes on into other dimensions and other levels of energy that are difficult to express on the physical plane. I can only give you analogies. You would be burnt to a crisp if you stayed too long, I'm afraid!

Have you met any interesting people since you've been over?

Oh, well, when you're on my level everybody seems to be interesting. You may have had a famous name whilst on the earth plane and some of the people even maintain an outward appearance for a while of particular lives that they've enjoyed, but they certainly wouldn't push themselves forward as being important people. The work is of course the really important thing.

Do you have any specific work?

Specific work? We don't really call it work. This is the difficulty again – loving people is not work, is it? If you really feel in love with someone you would not consider it work, but if you wish to call it work, The Work (in capital letters) is loving one another and coming to understand God's universe in whatever domain or level you happen to be on at the time. It is an onward going thing. It is infinite, as we've already expressed. You think you know everything when you're about six and it's only as you grow older that you realise there's always something else more to learn. It is a truly humble person if he becomes aware that he hardly knows anything in comparison to infinity. He may know a great deal more in comparison to other people on the earth plane but in comparison to infinity it is minuscule.

Would you know me and my life? I've been asked to teach eventually and perhaps use light trance. Is this the right way for me to go? Would you know that?'

I've met you in a soul way, I don't know you on a personal level. Each of us, as we meet, recognise each other as being a soul on the path, one who is awakening. If you wish to help your friends and fellow men in this way, if you have a really deep desire within your being and you have communicated with God upon this matter, then you are the only one really who can say whether you want to do it or not. I could say 'Oh yes, do it if you like', but if it does not go right and it goes wrong, you will blame me.

It's not that I mind being blamed at all. My shoulders are broad enough, but it is part of the spiritual path, learning to accept responsibility for your own decisions, and if you really feel this is what you would like to do I can assure you that it helps in little ways here and there, so long as you don't expect to get on the platform and command a great deal of attention. Then it can only be for your good and for other people's good, if you wish to channel the God energies. I don't wish to discourage you in any way whatsoever but you must look deep within yourself and not be pushed into it because of what other people have said. It has to come from your inner being absolutely.

Raynor, would it be that your coming to visit us is part of the work with capital letters?

Yes, The Work, yes. We're learning to love one another!

Do you have other groups who do the work?

Oh yes, yes. We work in slightly different ways of course. I do not speak through other people on this level, but I go to many groups and add my little bit. We try to communicate through telepathy and if people are trying to keep their minds quiet we try to help them by loving them; and possibly one or two people I have taken on as my responsibility I will try to point in the right direction when they ask. From the higher levels we are never allowed to impose. This is how you can discriminate again between those of a lower level who will tell you that you must do this and you must follow their instructions. This is one of the discriminative levels. On the higher levels you are always left with the ability to decide. It is rather like children. You tell them what to do when they're younger and you allow them, as they grow up and become more responsible, to make the decisions for themselves. If you do have someone telling you that you must do what they say under all circumstances then both you and the person concerned are on a lower level because you must be still a child and they must also be spiritually childlike, I would say.

Do you still discuss any philosophic questions?

Oh yes, there are many philosophical questions always being discussed. We do it with a great deal of love and a great deal of joy. We do not fight over the questions. Here again you have to learn to discriminate what is the truth, yes? Your level of truth may not be someone else's but it is seeking to find the absolute truth. This is the on-going business, if you like.

Do you still have any relaxations which we might call pleasures?

Oh, living is pleasure, my friend! I have my own little

idiosyncrasies. I like to dabble in a kind of painting but it is a mixing of colours with the mind. You can use an implement if you want to, but there are little practices that I like to do and I learn to manifest pictures that may bring other people pleasure or may inspire them to seek further within themselves for the inner God. I express in my pictures that which I have felt and seen, and in this way it perhaps gives somebody else an idea or an inkling of what I experience, and in this way you share.

Whenever you start your discourse it always seems applicable to whatever has just happened.

Yes, that's right. Well, of course, we are never really far away. The trouble with the physical plane is that we still think in terms of space, time and distance, whereas we are really only a thought away and if we feel that you are in trouble we can be with you in a moment. It is no problem. I think I explained before, it's rather like a telephone. If somebody is engaged you do not bother them, you ring again, you come again. You do not interrupt or interfere if a person is involved in a particular train of thought with someone, but if they are really shouting for help, we can keep an eye on you, in a sense, to see that you are pursuing the path and if you are not, we may try to send a little thought in your direction. But it's not so much thought in your sense, it is on a love energy. It is very definitely energy and all the time you are dissipating it, through too much talk, too much wasting time on unnecessary things. You virtually have to decide for yourselves what is necessary. I would not say to you you must not do this. It's only that I've already gone through it, that I realise that some of the things you think are necessary are not really, but this is part of your life, and at this point you may have to do some of the things that are not really necessary until you become aware that they are not really necessary after all. Quite often you have to go through some form of illness. You may have to go through a shock. Maybe someone close to you has died or is ill, and you realise time as you understand it in the physical body is limited. It is not that life itself is limited, by any means. There may be a kind of blanking off for a time until these little shocks wake you up, or wake others, to the fact that now is the opportunity, and to try and take the opportunity, instead of keeping on leaving it until tomorrow. You do have a few more tomorrows, my friends: do not worry, you are not about to pop off at any moment.

From spirit, I've heard from the platform, that I am wearing my grandmother's pearls and yet I've also been told that spirits only see your spirit self, they cannot see your bodies. What is the truth?

Well, the truth of the matter is that everything is energy, yes? And even though the physical is vibrating at a lower rate than the spiritual, it is still an energy and it still gives off light. We learn to be able to tell the different energies that we see. We learn to discriminate.

So the pearls would give off an energy?

Yes, yes!

Would the pearls, or a wedding ring, also have some of the energy of the person who wore it?

Yes, they have both the energy of the person who has worn it, or of the person who made it, or since pearls come from the sea, the energies from under the sea and everything appertaining to the sea. We learn to read that, like some people learn to read auras. You know when you first come into the world you don't fully understand what you're seeing, you see things but you don't really understand what they are. You hear things but you don't fully understand what they are, and as you grow you hear sounds – now don't you – without taking too much notice? You know what that sound is related to. Well it is rather like that for us if we see you, you understand?

I've been writing, feeling possibly some input from yourself there?

This is one of the ways we work with people through groups, and we work through story lines. This is how fairy stories come into being. There is much spiritual teaching in fairy stories, if you read between the lines, as there is in the Bible. As you meditate you become more aware of the inner truths. People who are not ready will just read it as a story but their inner self will register, if you understand, but not their conscious mind. And in a way this can be like a little seed sown so that should they become aware of the need to meditate the seed will be flushed with light and will grow as a plant.

Sometimes I get messages in words, sometimes they describe a picture. Now the person who is sending the information is able in some way to project a picture. I'm very interested in how it's done.

It's the thought. You have the television. It's rather like that, if you like. We send out thoughts in picture form, which are picked up by your spirit, or even passed on. If it is really important, and you need to know, then someone will put this picture in your mind. If they can't get this picture to you they will try to contact a more sensitive friend who will pass on the message. You say 'It's funny I was thinking about so and so just lately', or 'I had a dream'. That's another form of trying to pass the message on, because as a child you think in picture form anyway. It's only as we grow older that we learn to clothe the thought in words. The animals think in picture form. They see. We have some people, like the artist, who catches it, produces it in painting because they are better at visualising. You have other people who are better at writing because they have developed the intellectual aspects of their being and they have learned to understand the vibrations of words, the sounds of words. We try to express things with clarity. We have a little difficulty with the teeth and the tongue.

I'm sure the medium will not object to my expressing this. Maybe we could send love to each individual in the group. Perhaps you could have five minutes, so that each person can perhaps experience what it feels like to have other people's love given to them directly. If you could name them perhaps. This is only a suggestion, it is not my instruction. You again must learn to discriminate what you want to do and what you feel is the right thing to do, but it is a good exercise in concentration and it is for learning to become receptive and to allow the mind to rest. It may help you to visualise a kind of white watery bubble or an iridescent bubble, whichever is easiest, and think of love. My blessings.

FOUR

The God Within

We're not really sure exactly what is wanted of us. Perhaps you could enlighten us a little.

Well, always it is the God within that is essential. You need always to work toward that as your single goal, to become aware of the God within whilst on the planet, instead of waiting until you pass; to learn to be an alchemist, if you like, to change yourselves while you're here. This is a great opportunity to bring all these energies together while you're in the body and to bring it all under the control of the higher self. As I've said before, your psychic abilities will develop on the way, anyway, and if you wish to use them as a tool then this is very good.

Would you say there's a plan for the group and if so are we going along the right road?

Well, when we say there is a plan, it's very flexible. You know it's rather like your life, you're born and you die – well I say die – and there are the main points in your life that are going to happen, but there's a certain amount of flexibility because there are so many intricacies to do with yourselves and your lives. It's not very wise to make everything too hard and fast, too rigid, for it has to grow, do you follow? You will find it will become clearer in your lives individually, as you go along and try to take each – I was going to say each moment as it comes – but you can often use this idea within the group to take each afternoon that you meet as an individual moment in time, do you follow me? It's a little difficult to explain that, in a sense, you're trying to reach into the atmosphere of no time. We will try to convey this sense of timelessness to each of you individually so that you can experience it, whilst in between we will try and speak to you as well, or to pass other information that may be of use within your daily life because, let's face it, it is your daily life that is important. It is very good to want to save the planet but unless you're saving yourself at the same time people will say, 'It's all very well, but what are you doing with your life?' It is what you are radiating. If you are radiating joy and love people will want to know how you do it, how it is that you're coping with problems so peacefully. Are you doing this just yet? Do you follow me?

We try but we're not doing it exactly yet.

No, we understand, we know the difficulties but there is a Japanese saying, is there not, *'If everyone scrubs their door-step the whole village is clean.'* Do you follow? And just let us flow. Do not deny the creative thoughts in your own mind. Put them forward. Allow the creative thoughts through, don't block them all the time by saying, *'Oh that is just my imagination'*. Your imagining ability is God-given, your image-creating abilities have been given to you. You follow this? I think I'd better leave it on that note. We won't go into depths of things at the moment.

We want to feel that we are achieving some purpose or other in meeting, you know.

The purpose is to love one another, love one another and from that everything will grow. It is like the soil, once you plant the seed and water it with love, it will grow.

Thank you.

I say good afternoon. It is a little warm for you; I think you are in need of cups of tea. I will not hold you up.

Do you miss cups of tea?

On occasions I do, yes. Where would we be without the cups of tea?

Do you have time to answer a question please.

Yes, yes.

I've had a letter from Paul Beard and wondered if he might ask a personal question: he believes he had a rather discreditable life at the time of the Inquisition and he wondered if you and he were connected in any way at that time?

Yes. Remembering the Inquisition was bringing back some sadness to my memory and I hope that we have learned to forgive one another. As for my part I've asked for forgiveness and received it. Is there any more?

He said he had been waiting and waiting for the return of Raynor Johnson.

Perhaps he doesn't realise that I never really left him.

Perhaps he's realising it now.

FIVE

Letting the Light Shine

There is a great deal of talk these days about letting your light shine. This is not just an intellectual concept you understand, this is literal. In fact, by concentration of the mind to start with, you lift your vibrations and if you think of colour this can be seen, and the brighter your light the easier it is for us to see. This also lights the path for others who come in contact with you. They may not see it with their eyes but those who are on the spiritual path, wherever, will sense it. They will be drawn to you like a magnet draws a pin. In that way they can be drawn into your vibrations and you can, even without speaking, help that soul to come into tune with your vibrations because yours are the stronger. You know the analogy of the one clock and the other clocks all coming into time with it? It is something similar to that. It is obviously not exactly the same because we have this difficulty, you understand, of always trying to convey to you in your terminology that which we see. I understand this is partly why we are here, yes? We are not supermen or women, we are simply those who have gone on and are now living in that other dimension, or those other dimensions, which I understand you are reading about. Now you have expressed thoughts that you wish to help wherever you can within the limits of your own lifestyle or your own karmic patterns. In your meditations, think of the colours which you have read about and which you see. In your meditations, go through the colours of the chakras which some of you already do, and if you could devote a little more time to it, you will find that your vibrations will lift. You will find it much easier next time, so that when the need from some other soul has made itself known you will already be vibrating on that higher level. It is in a way trying to draw away from your everyday thoughts. You obviously have to deal with the practical things of life but each time there is a break in your everyday thoughts your attention should return to higher thoughts, again like the pin to the magnet. Your thoughts should be drawn back automatically if there is a gap in your thinking, instead of you wasting time going over the same monotonous worries, because I think we've all learned that by worrying we do not solve the problem. We have to give some thought to the problems in hand, but if it gets to the stage where you go over and over the same problem, just realise that is what *your* mind is doing, whereas your purpose is really that you are training your mind. You are bringing your mind under the control of your higher self, so that you are in control of the mind, not it in control of you. I realise I'm not telling you anything you don't already know but I thought it would be an introduction to my coming and we could go on from here. It is a bit like establishing the nature of the lessons you wish to share. I won't say I am giving it to you; I feel it is more a matter of sharing and drawing it together in a concentrated form so that we can go step by step and just clarify what it is you and I feel that we need to do. It is rather like when you first had to learn your numbers, yes? You had to learn to understand what the signs are, the symbols, but once that is established we can go on to greater things. Now I don't wish to put anyone down in any way. I do realise you're far beyond your numbers, but this is just again another little analogy. It is just a kind of drawing the threads together so that I understand what you think and you understand what I think. So if you are happy we can go on from there.

You've heard of mantras and things; you can teach yourself a certain sound. In India the teachers obviously give their pupils their specific sounds that they have for their specific pupils. Now you may have a certain sound that you prefer to use. I'm sure you could find some in many books, or you may hear one from your own guide. And if you do hear one, then you can use this particular sound. You can go back in habit. You can use these habit-forming abilities which are usually rather negative, but you can use them for constructive work also. Instead of waiting and letting the mind just drift, you can think of the sound or try to listen to the OM and it will draw you. Once you have established that pattern you won't have to work quite so hard at having to lift yourselves. The vibration will draw you up so that when you are quiet, you are at peace and not fretting. If you are waiting, you are waiting in an awareness that is you are where you are at the moment. You *become* a state of being. It is a little difficult ..... let me see now if I can grasp the words. There is a tendency, with human beings, that if something doesn't help immediately there is fretting?

Now, you could perhaps feel yourself in your own space so that the fretting goes on around you, not inside you. There is usually a reason why you have to wait and it is not always something you can do anything about. If you feel you can, or there is a need to, you can physically go and try and see what it is but it is keeping the fretting outside so that you are a single point of light which is at rest within. Now I know you are living in a world of change so there is constant movement, so in a way you have all this to contend with, but part of your reason for being here is learning how to be aware of God whilst in the dimension of change. Now what happens after the time you have all these thought patterns and vibrations bombarding you? It's rather like a planet or a spaceship with meteorites which come swarming past. The spaceship needs to have its protection to prevent it from being damaged by all these meteorites. In a way you are rather like spaceships, because you are really space with energy within you, and your bodies are a different form of spaceship, and your mind propels, but the energy is God, the source of the energy is God, it is the life force. You understand this, I know. To take it to the other extreme, you can develop the ability to travel to different dimensions and to different planetary energies whilst still in the body, or I should say connected to the body. But should you take this to the fullest, you become aware of the God within and this God-energy is everything and everywhere, and therefore you can travel without having to wait until your body has disintegrated. I think some of you may have experienced this already.

So it's not imagination, though you're not sure.

That's right, yes. This is like dreaming, you think it is real and it is real to you. It is only when you come back that it seems fantastic or a fantasy, but the more you experience this the more you will be able to bring the memory back as you develop – evolve I think is the more correct terminology.

Really and truly we can talk and we can talk, and you can listen and you can listen, but it's not the same as experiencing, is it?

So all we can do when we come is to try to tell you our experiences, share with you our experiences and knowledge and try to lift our vibrations, and ask each other questions, and different teachers, of course, like everyone else, have their individual experiences. So there may at times seem to be contradictions, as in the analogy of going up the mountain. Two people on either side of the mountain will swear blind that the view is such and such a thing and they will be correct, but it is only when you get to the top and you can both see everything that you realise that you were both correct but you did not have the whole picture. So try to keep an open mind even when people tell you something that is totally contradictory. I don't mean you have to accept it. There's nobody asking you to be fools. One has to use one's intelligence.If you can, just leave it. If you can just let it go through your mind and out the other side if it is not for you do so. Try not to get drawn in to the negative which can be brought to anything. If you get too negative instead of lifting, you'll be pulling yourself and others down. You will not be doing anyone any good. Now I understand this is also, again, very difficult because we all enjoy a little chit-chat and the negative is very powerful. It can disguise itself as seemingly being constructive when in fact you can actually feel the energies coming down. If you find that people are conversing on a negative, the vibrations drop and you can see the light go dim. I expect some of you can feel this.

You understand this feeling that some people are rather like vampires. That is how these stories came about. People are like vampires to one another. They do draw you down into their negativity. So if you can build this light around you they can bombard you as much as they like but it will not affect you. In fact it may even cast a little light upon them so that they will be drawn to thinking, or to being aware, that this person is stronger than they are and they may even question why. There is always this possibility that you can help somebody in this way but be very careful that you don't get drawn into their argument. Let them rabbit on. It doesn't bother you.

We say we raise or lower our vibrations – what is it that vibrates?

It's rather like saying 'What is God?' I'm watching to see if I can see the patterns. Now we talk about atoms, the subatomic particles, yes? Well this obviously has to do with this dimension. All I can see and understand, at my level of understanding, is energy. You can see movements of energy but it is a little difficult to understand what it actually is. All we understand is that it is the life force, the God within. We try to explain it but we cannot. All we can do is experience it and when we do, it depends again on what level we are experiencing it. So I could say to you that within my band of experience it is this, but you go to another level of another band and they would describe it as something entirely different. But whatever it is, it seems to get finer and finer and there is a feeling of refinement, of cleanliness, of utter, utter ...

Purity?

But you don't really know what it is, what the purity is. All you know is that it is wonderful,. All I can say for myself is that it is experienced as love, seen as light. I'm being given the pyramid shape and it is as though it comes to a finer state of purity, of being.

Sometimes those who visit us are not anxious to give their names. Is there a special reason for this?

It is just that some of us have had famous incarnations

and some of us have had quiet incarnations, working unseen. It is that in some cases it could be taking more notice of us because of the name rather than what we say, yes? And we are also inclined to put aside self; and again the mediums are human and many can gain egotistical pleasure from using a name, and can get carried away by the name rather than the teachings. The teachings are given freely. If they are not acceptable each of us has the freedom to accept or reject. I, for myself, would not wish anyone to take notice of myself if it was totally against their reasoning mind. We have been given the intelligence..... we are the intelligence that is the higher energy. Intelligence is different from fact-gathering.

The mind that just gathers fact just gathers information. It does not necessarily mean it is intelligence. Intelligence is another thing altogether. It is intelligence that selects and can tell which is for its good and which is not. I can give you a name which is one that would serve for this moment but again we can choose names as we wish, in the same way that you can choose your names. You have been given a name by your parents, but you can choose another name. Obviously, it is easier if you stick to one name so that your friends know who you are, but then again it is not just your name that they recognise you by. They recognise you by your essence and by the way you look, the way you sound, by your mannerisms.

Do you transmit your words as words or as thoughts through the medium?

We have come through the medium. In this situation where the medium is conscious but had to learn to put aside her own thinking processes temporarily, we have to use the mind, but again we are using thought. You have to use thought. It is only through thought that I can actually convey to you that which is coming through the medium's mind in the present.

Are you limited by the vocabulary that's available?

Oh yes, yes. This idea where people think they need not learn anything, therefore it is going to be more truthful when the spirit speaks, is not necessarily so. We have found that in fact it helps us if the medium has read a great deal and has had an adequate education. We sometimes have to work quite a long time with the medium – for many years – without their always realising. We lead them to read different books, to expand their vocabulary or the subjects that they study and think about. If they have had some thought on the subjects it makes it so much easier for us to speak. So we try to lead you perhaps to different teachers on the earth plane, or to friends with whom you can share a conversation on a particular subject. We will try to draw you together, without force, for we are not allowed to force anyone and obviously if the person is not going to be interested then we would let them go their own way. All we can do is influence. We do not seek to dominate anyone. That is more for the negative, the people on the lower levels, and this is the danger on the lower levels: that the ones who try to dominate are the ones who are not good for you. It's again rather as on a human level. You often get people who are aggressive and very dominating but they're not necessarily speaking sense at all. The most arrant nonsense can be said in an authoritative manner and it is often the quiet ones who are the thinkers and who could, in fact, help society if it would but listen. But you know yourself it is difficult. You get the noisy ones who will make such a loud noise and lesser ones tend to listen. You see this in your wars. Think how much easier it could be. But then you know there is room for all kinds. You have to remember that the earth planet is here as a learning experience. There's a place for everyone.

Do you choose a medium who speaks the language with which you were familiar when you were incarnated?

Not necessarily, not necessarily, no! It is easier but no, not necessarily.

Occasionally a medium will speak a few phrases in a foreign language which that medium could never have known. Are you in some way perhaps using sounds to come through?

I think that's a totally different technique there. I understand that the sort of mediums who go deeply unconscious are in fact drawn out of the body slightly, not completely, slightly, so that the control can come in and then use their minds. This is a somewhat different technique. It is not one I'm very familiar with. I have been more interested in being drawn to mediums who are aware. We feel that it is necessary for the medium to share in whatever is happening, not at the time but in listening to the tape machine afterwards. Let's see if I can get some more information on this sort of business. We have those around us who are aware of other subjects and they can sometimes channel in that information whilst the medium is under the control of a different spirit entity. Yes, it is almost as though the human entity is removed slightly from the physical body; it's a bit like taking a stopper out, and although the spirit being superimposes, it is as though they can use the voice box to create these other sounds. It's almost rather like doing some kind of a bypass of the conscious part of the medium and in that way they seem to be able to speak these foreign languages. For what purpose would one want to do this, if no-one understands what you're saying? Unless it is evidence for people to say 'Ah yes! It must be spirit because the medium knows none of this language.' To certain people this would be impressive. Some people are more interested in that aspect of spirit and spirit workings. Does this help at all?

Is it a long time, in our terms, since you were formerly in incarnation?

Not too long ago, not too long ago, not in hundreds of years.

And do you know if you will return to the earth?

In a separate physical body I take it you mean?

Yes indeed. Thank you for the correction.

I feel I've never really left! Having done quite a lot of work whilst I was here it was in communication that I was interested so that I was able really to continue this work almost immediately I passed over. So in a way I've never really left the earth plane in that sense. Obviously I don't stay here all the time but at the moment I have no plans to return in a physical body, but those who are our guides, on the other levels, will have it in mind. I'm not in too much of a hurry at present!

Can you tell us anything of what you do when you're not talking to us here?

Ah ! It is unfortunate that we're really encouraged to say we have come to talk about spirit things and then having been asked a personal question ..... Well obviously there is much travelling that can be done. One can visit any place that one can be drawn to within the specific levels. I can also learn. I can go to lectures or meetings or just gatherings of friends, in much the same way as you do. You, on earth, can go out of the house and you can mix with people who do not think the same as you do – to do with spirit – but you all have your similar needs, you need home, you need clothes, you need friends, but on the levels that we're on there is a closer link obviously because we are in spirit. But again we can choose to be with certain friends and to communicate, and there are the bigger meetings, of course, where we all gather together when the entities of Beings from the higher levels come. This you know. Again I have not gone far enough beyond that to be able to tell you much else, but it is a wonderful experience, and as far as I'm concerned it is a very great highlight of my day. Again I use the word 'day' carefully.

Yes, I understand.

We can rest if we want to, if we need to be quiet. We don't actually shut people out but it is a kind of closing down so that if anyone wishes to communicate with us they're aware that we're not available. I dare say you find yourself, if you try any telepathy or communications on the other levels, there are times when the person you wish to speak to, or communicate with, is immediately there, but other times, well, they just don't seem to be available telepathically, yes? I don't know if any of you have tried this at all?

Maybe a smaller incident is when you wish to telephone someone and they telephone you instead. Well, it is very similar to that. We don't actually have answerphones but a similar principle works. This is why it manifests on the physical because there is something on the other levels.

I understand that your spirit body is a replica or similar to one that you had on earth. Does it contain any of the organs which would be necessary on earth to sustain life?

Strangely enough, yes. Yes, your heart beats and you breathe lightly. Yes, we do have replicas.

But you're not eating and drinking as we do?

No, no, strange isn't it? We haven't quite worked it out either!

I dare say we shall find out at some stage as to why, or maybe we don't have any of these organs at all when we get higher, but obviously the closer we are to the earth levels the nearer we are, because when you come to the earth it is a replica of what we have, not the other way round. We are not replicating you, you are replicating us, or we replicate ourselves when we come down.

We definitely need these organs down here.

Oh we do, don't we, yes. I get the impression that our organs actually have a similar sort of function but obviously not .....

With the same material?

We don't have to go to the toilet and things like that. That is all left behind but the body does channel and refine the energies that you use and it comes through you but instead of the waste being given out in the same way, here it is transmuted. Can you understand? It is not given out as a negative. It is cleansed before it comes out in some strange way. I've not quite learned how yet. In a sense, while you have your nurses and your doctors who go deeply into biology, the rest of you may have an inkling in varying degrees. We are rather like that, we have an inkling in some degree and we go deeper into it in other levels. If we wish, we can concentrate on learning exactly how it works. In fact I think I may well decide to look deeper into this. This is where I mean we can help each other. You can help me and I hope I can help you in some little way; even if it is just sharing my own experiences. I don't think I am that far – I'm not above you in any way; I'm just simply without a physical body and my memory of my experiences is a little clearer.

Can I ask – I've read in a book written from spirit where it was said by spirit that most of his sustenance came from breathing rather than eating, although he could eat if he wished. Is that how you find it?

Yes. When you first pass over obviously your memory of eating is still very clear and for those who still feel the need the food is provided and the drink, cups of tea, wine. When you find they no longer need that, the need just simply drops away. Nobody puts them on a diet or says you must not. They just find that they no longer think about it and they realise that the energy is being ..... they have been sustained in another way. It is only perhaps when they start to think about it that the information comes to them or they can be guided to other people who are also interested and want to know why, or they can then be led to a teacher. It isn't just through breathing. It seems to interpenetrate. The cosmic energies are all around, you are in it, you are of it. On certain levels it takes a form because you, as a consciousness, never completely disappear and you draw to yourself the particular particles of this energy that you require and it takes the form. You can change the form if you wish.

You know if you decide to be dressed and clothed in a certain apparel you can do so just by thinking, but if you wish to change your hair and your age, not your actual age, you just change the effect. To a certain extent we're rather like actors. You see what I mean? I can put on this act, you understand? Now in a way everyone does that even on this plane. It's just that you've got used to being that particular actor! Then you are shaped by your experiences and what you do with them. Does that help?

Could you alter your stature or your physique?

You mean size, yes? Oh yes, I can be enormous but in a way I have to ..... if I'm coming here ..... you know the expression putting the pint into your half pint?

Yes.

It's rather like that, concentrating the mind down so that you become centred more closely.

SIX

Trust

It is time I was allowed to speak on a subject that is dear to
my heart. Now we all realise how difficult it is to trust, do we
not? To put the trust in one's self is difficult because deep
within ourselves we are well aware that we do not have all
the answers. But we try to think things out by using our
intellect. Quite often we don't know what the absolute truth
is. Can we trust ourselves with our decision? Many times we
are held back by this lack of trust within ourselves, because
we have not touched on that deeper part of ourselves, which
is God. When you are in touch with your inner self, your
deep Godliness, then you can put a great deal more trust in
your decision knowing that if you do the best – if you have
weighed all the pros and cons, even if you make a mistake,
there are lessons to be learnt; there will always be something
to react to, and from which you can learn. This helps also in
learning to trust other people. You know you cannot trust
everyone but if you are putting your trust in the God within

yourself you realise that you do not have to defend yourself from the other person. You do not have to keep up your guard all the time. You do not have to live a fearful life, because it is yourself that you are really afraid of and not others. It is your reaction to what others do to you. If it is your reaction to what other people say to you, it is your ego that is doing the reacting, pride and insecurity or things like that.

If you are in touch with the God within, you will be in touch with other people's God within, and again I repeat, you will have less necessity to lift the barriers to protect yourself because the God within will give you whatever protection you need because you have put your trust in God. The rest is like building your house on the quicksand. This is a very familiar thing, is it not? It's very true. If your decision is based on other people's opinions, other people's opinions change and it is a bit like spitting in the wind, it invariably comes back and hits you in the face. Do you follow?

Excuse my little joke. If you dig deep enough into yourself you will make contact with other souls. It is your soul that needs to come to the fore. The self, the little self, which always wants to talk about itself, which always needs to mention itself, which always needs to be foremost in everything, is rather like having a small child with you. When you have a small child with you it always wants your attention. It wants to hold your hand, it always wants you to look at this and that and listen here. It distracts you all the time, does it not? The child tries to get you to follow it in a kind of butterfly manner, flitting from flower to flower. Well, if you watch your own minds, you will find that that little 'I' will have you doing the same sort of thing. It will try to distract you from deep thought and from deep meditation. Do not put your trust in this little child, which is yourself, but be compassionate with it. Do not indulge in great depths of guilt. Just acknowledge the fact that the child within will be with you for a little while yet but be kind to yourself, be kind. In other words do not send yourself into a dungeon of despair. If you do that you will not see your light and it will not help you at all. Just put it to one side, as you would a child, give it something to play with, but try to be in contact with that God within yourself and know that you can trust. If you make that link-up every day and every night and then go forward in whatever new decision you have made, knowing that something will come from it, and be ready to learn and to listen so that you will know, you will have this knowledge. You will have this knowing. All I can say to you really is keep on trying. I know there will be many days when you will want to give up. You'll think you can never concentrate, you can never get your mind to keep still long enough. You are well aware of the failings within yourself, and these are often reflected in the failings of other people. This is another way in which you can become aware that the little self has to be curtailed. But again be kind to yourself. There is no need to thunder away. This deafens out the friends who want to help you. They are there but you must ask for help if you are struggling. We will channel as much light as we can in your direction but if you put up the walls it will not help. We have to stand back and allow you to mull around in your own darkness until you've had enough, until you remember to ask for help. Remember to sit in the quietness and to trust that the great intelligence, that great creative force which is God and which is everywhere, does not exclude you in any way. It cannot exclude you. You are part of the life force. Allow this life force to radiate. Try to remember the light wherever you go. Try to think of love. If you hear yourself giving a condemning thought to someone, back it up by a channel of light. Do not be put off by your negative thought. Follow it up with a positive one but recognise what you're doing. You will eventually be able to do this all the time. Then you will experience the great joy and that great love that is God here and now, whilst on the earth plane. You will not have to wait until you pass over, and when you do pass over you will go straight into the light and not have to meander around on the lower realms.

It's very difficult to know when one has actually reached this God within. How does one know?

The joy within is the absolute recognition, but I do realise that until that point comes, the light almost comes through filtered. You have to just make the positive thought that this is what you want to do, and then put your trust in God, until that point where you can experience the joy and the love at all times. This is what I mean about learning to trust. You have a brain, your mind is the real you, you must use your mind through your brain to instruct your personality. Do you follow? Give it the instructions that this is what you want to do and then trust that if you do this daily the joy and the love will come through and your knowledge and your knowing will be absolute in time.

Do we get glimpses of it now and then and are we beginning to get towards it when suddenly we have a feeling of great happiness but don't know why? Is that the sort of thing you mean?

That is it, yes. It's almost as though one is partially illumined in little portions until the full illumination comes. Yes, you have these – we use the analogies. Sometimes it's rather like reaching the top of the mountain briefly and you have a grand vista of everything and then you have to take that back with you down the mountain and the memory sustains you and you keep on doing this until you are totally enlightened.

Recently I said to a minister of religion that in healing I try to make the God-self in me touch the God-self in the person that needed healing, but he didn't seem to really understand what I was saying at all.

No, unfortunately many ministers are closed in by the structures of the religious orders. They have set patterns of thought that they teach to students of religion and unfortunately many are afraid to open their minds to other kinds of thought. I'm not saying that this is for everyone. There are some ministers who do see a little further afield and still stay within the bounds of the Church and try to work from there, but many of them are followers rather than leaders, and they feel safer within their dogma. You are correct in your instructions there. I hope perhaps the gentleman may have learnt something from you. If not he may have gone away and thought about it.

He asked me what God said to me and I said that I didn't find God really saying anything to me in that sense, as a Being apart from me, and he found that very difficult to understand. In fact I think he considered it blasphemous.

Oh yes, God is supposed to be so far away that he cannot possibly have anything to do with us. This is an unfortunate teaching that has gone on for many aeons of time and kept many souls locked in fear. It is time for the light to manifest through the children and unfortunately many souls, like your minister maybe, will have to come back again and again.

It traps them in the circle of reincarnation?

Oh yes.

So if we could loosen that, would more souls go forward and break from the reincarnation cycle?

You must not try to shape them yourself. Just radiate the power and the light and let the light do the work. You may be led to say something to the person but you will have said it in a loving manner, whatever way they take it will be their karma. If they take it in a negative fashion that is their problem for them to solve, so long as you have given it out in love and not in a desire just to stir them up.

So the idea of God being within us is the great difference that might release a lot of souls if they only knew it?

Yes, yes.

The kingdom of heaven is within you.

Again that analogy of the fish swimming around in the water and asking where the water is brings to mind many little souls; that that is what they're doing. They do not realise that they are existing in light and that light exists within them; it's rather as though they're in a dark bottle.

Do you see an increase of spiritual awareness on the planet or do things remain much the same?

Yes, there is more of a spiritual awareness. Unfortunately when the light is more powerful there is also a greater stirring up of the negative. Instead of it staying in pockets in a kind of stagnant form it stirs up these energies, rather like when you get a wind blowing, it stirs up the atmosphere wherever it is and temporarily brings all the negative to the surface. It often seems as though it is getting worse from the material point of view, from the physical point of view, but this is not necessarily so on the spiritual. The light shines and shows up all the dark corners that need cleaning and clearing. Our minds are rather like this – the light shines in, and instead of feeling wonderful we are often more aware of how many more failings we seem to have, and one seems to be further away from the light than you thought you were originally, but this is only temporary. You have to be able to see the dirt to be able to clear it up. If you do not see what is hidden in the dark corners of your mind you will never be able to change, but if you're aware of it, that's half the battle. And you may find that you overreact to certain things, which is possibly what is happening again to our new friend who is not with us. The light is stirring her up and possibly making her more volatile. But give her time, give her time, she will be all right.

When groups like this come together have they often had any previous connections?

Oh yes, yes. We make links time and time again as we go along the path. We have usually met before. There is a sense of recognition, not always knowing where or when, but there is a soul recognition when you meet. You may not even speak, you may just be passing in the road, on the bus, in the car, you will have a feeling – do any of you remember doing this, meeting people and you just feel you know them? Does that happen often? Not to that depth, but there are others that you may briefly touch? Because you have all got a great deal of work to do in various parts of the planet and you would not really have time to all link up on the personal level and, anyway, that is not the aim. The aim is to link up soul-wise. The aim is to try to put the little self quietly to one side. You follow? Just observe how many times during the day you mention 'I', just as a small exercise for perhaps a day, just see how many times. Don't get bothered if you do, just recognise that you have mentioned 'I'.

Writing letters – how many times one puts 'I'.

There is this fear, is there not, that if you do not have strong opinions, if you do not voice them you will be turning into a nonentity, yes? There is this feeling you may go through for a little while but this is allowing space for the light to fill. Do you follow this? If you allow the God within to come to the fore you will radiate more power than you will ever experience, far more than the personality will ever be able to do. Your opinions are only based on a few facts. Everyone's opinion is only based on a few facts. You may in fact have had the experience that everyone has decided to have an opinion about you, and you didn't realise people thought about you like that, and you realise how far from the truth they are. And when you think about it, even you do not know all the facts in every situation you find yourself in. If you are interacting with someone else you do not know everything that the other person has experienced. You only know your portion and, if you are basing your decisions on opinions, including other people's opinions, you will find that there will be some pitfalls into which you could fall and from which you could possibly learn. I do not wish to frighten anyone! This can be quite amusing at times so long as you keep your sense of humour to the fore. Enjoy laughing at yourself. This allows the joy through, you see. You do often find that that which seems the most disastrous to the personality can be extremely amusing.

How does what you have said link up with the 'I am' idea?

Are you thinking of the meditation on 'I am'? I think you are touching on your soul self when you think of the 'I am'. It has many connotations. There is the surface 'I am', the 'I am' of the everyday, but if you take it deeper you will find that the 'I am' is.

Is what?

Is! It is a state of being, it is a state of being now. Not I am in the past or I am in the future; I am now, I am everywhere, I am all. Try to experience in your meditation for yourself. You may hear my words but as I have said before it is always second-hand if you hear it from another, but if you experience it yourself, in your meditation, you will find it will lead you into a more profound state of consciousness.

And is that a way of getting in touch with God and in trust?

Yes.

So do you feel like my teacher who says that the 'I am' is recognising the soul?

Yes, because the soul is part of God. You will be able to observe the difference between the 'I am' of the everyday personality. It is part of learning to discriminate, as part of your learning is to discriminate. This is not to say I was passing judgement.

A little problem we often have.

Only a little one.

I see what you think. We say, 'Judge not lest ye be judged', and yet every move in life requires some judgement. Is it possible perhaps to judge without condemning, in order to make plans, make arrangements, decide on partners, etc?

Yes, this is a difficult one. When you're passing judgement do you consider it the same as making an assessment?

It is done, or it should be done, if it's going to be done at all, without any of the negative. If you can assess everything with a joyful heart you are in no danger. Should you judge, and you are not judging with a joyful heart, you are laying yourself open for quite a few more lessons. So should you wish to continue judging you are free to do so!

So do what you like and pay for it!

Precisely. I say this with tongue in cheek because if you still feel the need to do this by all means ..... but be careful.

So would that then be the 'judge not' thing, so that the 'ye be judged' would be the karma?

Yes, yes, that's right. If you judge somebody on something they've done or said, without knowing all the facts or knowing their soul path, you may find yourself in very much the same situation, with someone judging you in the same way that you have judged them. If you are in a difficult situation and you are unhappy, ask yourself what sort of friend would you really like to have with you – someone who judges your situation or someone who listens with a loving heart? So try to apply that which you find within your meditations to your everyday life and to other people's problems. Listen but – it is a very difficult path to follow, I'm not saying it is easy – if you're really being drawn to helping others, then one of the very difficult things to do is to listen without passing judgement or thinking 'I wouldn't have done it this way', or 'I would never have got into that situation'.

Plenty to think of, yes? I will leave you now and let you have a little time to think, to think on me and I leave you with God's blessings and thank you for having me.

SEVEN

The Spiritual Path

There are three aspects of the spiritual path that I would like to speak to you about this afternoon. The first is the spiritual purpose in your life, the second is the spiritual character, and the third is your spiritual realisation. These three aspects are usually developing at the same time in varying degrees, depending on what experience you are having at any moment, how the divine purpose in your life has to come into your conscious mind, which is the real reason why you have taken a physical body in this dimension. Most people do not really consider this matter until they are in their thirties and possibly they may ask themselves 'Why am I here?' These are perhaps the first beginnings and questionings, maybe after some traumatic experience, and after many thoughts and discussions with people they may eventually become aware that the purpose they have is divine; a divine purpose for being in their physical body. In the meantime your character is developing. You are having your experiences. You are acting and reacting to the different situations you find yourself in and by trying to bring forward the good within yourself you will develop your divine character. This again is the higher self being brought into the conscious mind, acting through your personality. The working of the divine purpose and the divine character will bring you to divine realisation. You have many small realisations. This is like a curtain being drawn away from your mind, you could say. It is the sudden ability to realise something you did not see before. Do you follow? This is why it is called realisation. It is realising that which is within, the truth that is there within yourself, the light, the love, the knowledge. All this has possibly been channelled in varying degrees through your personality and through your various existences in different dimensions whilst you are in time. But the divine purpose is for you to come to that full realisation whilst you are in the physical body, this physical body you have been allowed to take. There are many souls waiting for physical bodies so, no matter how hard your life, it is actually a privilege for you to be allowed to use some other person's body for you to come into the womb and be given birth. Your mother has accepted the responsibility and no matter how good or how bad the mother, she has given you a great gift for which you can give thanks to God.

I do realise that at times when life is troublesome it is very difficult to give thanks but even in the troublesome times – I say even, but I should say that in spite of the troublesome times – you can learn a great deal and quite often it is through the troublesome times that you can actually learn more. You can develop the compassion that will come through as divine character and your inner trust will grow until you have a full realisation of what your true purpose in life is and so we come back again to divine purpose. It is like going round and round in a circle in a sense, which is symbolic of infinity. Do you follow?

It seems so simple when you put it into words, doesn't it? But so difficult actually to put into practice. I give you just a short discourse as you have had quite a long time with your exercise. If you could persist in this exercise you would find that your inner consciousness would develop that much quicker. It would help to make you more sensitive, and help to clarify the thoughts you have. It would clear away some of the dross. It will help you to see the reality of all situations that you are in, and that other people are in, who come to you with their problems. You will know immediately what their problems are and what the source of their problem is. Of course, this does not mean that you will be able to help them. I think you have all reached the age of discretion? Even our young one here.[1] She may be young in body but she is old in soul. She has been on this path many, many aeons of time and has come this time to do what she can, for which we give thanks. And we understand that you are all giving in your own way. But, my friends, you have to give in God's way. You have to come to that point in your life when you must make it God's way. I say 'must' but no-one is forcing you. You understand? It is your own choice. You have made this choice or you would not be listening to my words now. This does not mean that I am an extra special person, it simply means that I am a little step further on from yourselves, possibly because I am in another dimension. Do you follow?

Yes.

There is none of us above the other, only in the amount of love and light that we can give to our fellow beings. This is

---

[1] A young woman who ran a Spiritual Health Centre had recently joined the circle.

how God works through us all. Do not allow the little moanings of the personality to drag you down. I repeat it again and again each time I come. They can be very troublesome, can they not?

EIGHT

Death as a Doorway

As you can see, death is only a doorway into the next dimension. Most of the time it is simply a word we use to describe something we don't know anything about until, of course, somebody helps us with the information or we have the experience ourselves, or a memory of it. We prefer to think of it as a doorway rather than the end and you can obviously see why. If someone has a traumatic death they do need help. If someone passes in sleep they are resting when they pass over, or they may already be with friends on the other side who have come to them and taken them in their dream state. It is easier, of course, to leave your body if you are older, because you start to loosen your holds on your physical body the older you get. It is very difficult for young people, it can be very traumatic for them, particularly if they have not considered life after death. They do not always realise quite what has happened and we need to talk to them quietly and explain. Those who have left families behind, particularly young children, can of course be upset. It is not necessarily a happy passing immediately. It is only perhaps having gone for a rest and then been awakened later that they realise that they can see their children, or meet their children while the children are in their dream state. So in fact they are not totally parted from them. They will of course be a little concerned for them on immediately passing, wondering about the little details of who is going to take care of the child's needs or its little habits. But this soon passes and the peace and joy fills their heart and mind and they realise they have not lost touch with their families. There is much work for us to do on this side when people pass into the next dimension, like our friend here[1]. She has been taken care of, there are two beings of light who came by her side and were with her all the time. So she was in no further danger from any other negative vibes from your dimensions. I feel that I am now in the lower dimensions at the moment and sometimes it feels as though I am still partaking of the same vibrations as yourself. It is very difficult to talk to people, is it not, about the word 'death'. People tend to pull away from you if you wish to talk about it.

When all you want to do is pass on some good information and extend your welcome to them, they are afraid. This you will have to consider all the time when you are discussing it with people. It is a fear that they have to overcome. It is rather like a dark hole to them. You are, in a word, whipping the carpet from under their feet, particularly if they have very definite views about what death is, and no matter how faulty the information that they have, it is the only view that they will cling to. So try to understand their reluctance at first and just persist gently. In many cases you

---

[1] A lady who made contact through another medium present

have to wait, I am afraid, and just approach them on the inner levels, through the mind, through the power of your mind, and by doing this on the inner levels you will be able to develop your powers of concentration. You will be very surprised at yourself at times, and how you will be able to hold someone in your mind and fill them with light.

This will be good for you when you do pass over yourselves because, instead of moving around quickly rather like a ball, you will be able to be more stable immediately you have passed over. I cannot say to you that everything takes place in a specific way when you pass over into the different dimensions because as you probably realise there are many aspects of living. In the same way if someone landed on your earth planet they would not always realise that they were in the same place on the same earth, because it is so different. It is like that in the different dimensions. We try to guide each soul to that with which they are familiar.

There they can rest and take their time to assimilate their surroundings. It is later on that they can either choose to work as we do, or they can work with the different dimensions, or they can develop talents that they already had, or even satisfy some desires they may still have with them. There are the dimensions where you can satisfy any desires but of course it is better for you, if you are on a spiritual path, to try to go beyond the dimensions of desires. You are aiming for the dimension where all is as it should be. I cannot describe that dimension – that is way beyond my powers – but once you reach that level you will have no need to come back to any earth planetary system at all.

Are you more conscious of the Divine than you were when you were on earth?

I am, yes.

Can I ask how this expresses itself, how you're conscious of it?

The joy, the love and a feeling of being expanded. There is not that sense of limitation that you have in the physical body. You do not feel alone, you cannot feel alone while you're filled with love and joy and the sharing of energies.

Do you find there are realms which you cannot yet approach, that you'll have to wait until you have made sufficient progress to go to these realms?

Oh yes. There are even brighter realms than we are on already. We are allowed to draw close and to a certain extent the boundaries overlap so that we may visit for very short periods of time in the company with those Beings who live on that level. They will protect us from being overcharged by the energy. Do you follow? And then we return back to our own dimension that much more uplifted and encouraged to go on. Many people choose to stay on one dimension for many aeons of time but, if you're meditating, you're learning from meditation that it is possible to experience many of the levels of awareness through the power of your own mind. You realise that you can expand and that you can feel other people and other Beings without actually touching each other physically. It is like that in our dimension also, only to a greater degree.

That's very interesting. Thank you very much. Are you conscious of more than one time where you are or just the time of your own region?

I do not think we could call it 'time' in the sense that you would understand. There is no particular clock ticking away telling us that we have only a minute left. In a way I can only tell you what there is not. It all seems to do with vibrations and tuning in and of being aware. These are only words that I can use to try to give you an idea; and the only other way that you could understand what I mean is to experience it in your meditations. We are beyond time. It is only when you have a birth and a death and you have seasons, when you have a growing old and a coming in with the new, that you can regulate your time, otherwise how would you know that time had passed anyway?

I know it seems a terribly simple question but does one thing happen after another?

Many things happen at once, they just seem to happen one after another, because there is not the time factor. You can be aware of many things happening or going on around you at the same time but you can focus on one thing at a time if you choose. In a way it's rather like having many television sets in the room all with different programmes on, or channels. You can either stay in the middle and assimilate them coming from all directions, or you can focus your mind on one of them and should you wish to recap on one that was going on in another dimension you can, in a way, re-run it, in the way that you re-run your videos. It can be recorded for you in your own mind. It doesn't mean that somebody outside yourself is recording it or rerunning it, it is just something that you can do, but we do not have this time factor to bother with. It is only when we come back to this dimension that we have to try to focus, or pinpoint, down. It's rather like losing a certain amount of our extended awareness so that we can focus into this particular point that we have come to. This is why sometimes I have to stop to listen to what someone on my dimension is saying to me because it is difficult for me to control the body of the medium and communicate with you and keep my extended awareness at the same time. So I hope you will excuse me if I do not seem so Godlike!

Do you use words in the realm in which you are or do you use thoughts?

Thoughts.

My friends on your side have been trying to make me think faster. Instead of my stopping and putting all the words to it they're trying to stop me immediately after the thought has arrived, and get used to accepting it all in one go. Am I right to do that?

Yes, because putting it into words can sometimes take so long. If you can assimilate it in the form in which they are giving it to you that is better for you. But of course you may at some other time have to try and put it into words for other people; in that way they will help you.

Do you remember speed reading at all when you were here? Well, they say they're teaching me speed thinking.

It is a little bit like that of which I am speaking. The analogy of the television set is very crude but it perhaps gives you an idea of what I mean and I think you are following up with your own experiences.

If I am driving the car and my mind has jumped a gear and I'm floating off with all different ideas, is there somebody actually tuning in the whole time with me about what I'm thinking about, what I call shallow thoughts, not concentrating and meditating?

There are different levels of thought working. You can drive your car, can't you, without really thinking too much about it? Yet you are driving accurately. That is one level. With the next level perhaps you observe the scenery. And then there are the other levels to do with people who are not around. You could also, on this level, pick up other people's thoughts around you, the other people that are connected with you on this level, and there are other levels where your guide will be trying to help you through your daily work and protect you from any accidents or whatever. If nothing untoward is about to happen they will just send you loving thoughts, and there are other levels of thought which you may touch on while you're in the body but at different times.

Now if you're meditating you are beginning to open these channels more so you may find yourself drifting off. Do be careful if you find yourself doing too much of that when you're driving. Try to shut yourself down a little more if you do find yourself tending to do that to the detriment of your driving, but it is good that you are extending into these other dimensions. It is part of your learning process.

Am I going on to the right spiritual pathway?

First meditate and contact your inner God, that is the first and foremost, and from that you will be led in different directions to experience different lessons. Your own inner self, with your guide, especially with your guide, will impress upon you to do this and to do that. You'll meet certain people where you will have your different experiences and from these experiences try to learn what it is about yourself that you need to know. That way you will come to understand other people on deeper levels. Be honest with yourself. You don't have to admit any of your faults to anyone else. They are your business. You have your good points, we all know that, but unfortunately it is the negative aspect that usually needs clearing up and in which we are less interested. I have the same problems. This negative aspect of ourselves tends to trip us up here and there but unfortunately when we get into a negative way of thinking it tends to go round in circles and we forget that we are supposed to be looking at these negative aspects to see what part of ourselves is giving us trouble. It is usually some aspect of pride.

Have you met any people that you particularly admired when you were on earth?

The name Bertrand Russell comes to mind. We have many discussions on philosophy here. We have such fun in disagreeing.

Is he still of the opinion .... ?[2]

Oh, he still has many opinions! Many of which he is reluctant to give up.

He could hardly be materialistic, could he?

Not now! But we enjoy ourselves. We do it in love knowing that there are many opinions that we have to let go, I'm afraid.

I am concerned that many tragedies are impending on earth, many people will pass, we understand, and a great deal of work will be necessary in your world to meet the people coming over. Does this present some form of crisis to people who organise this?

Yes, it does, but here are many willing helpers. Yes, do not worry yourself too much, but your thought has been noted. Just send your love and any energies that you feel you have to spare will be taken up. We have many centres. They're rather like batteries, if you like, and they take the forms of pyramids, pyramid shapes. They glow with light. They accumulate energies and this energy can be used by anyone drawing close to the earth. It's rather like being a deep-sea diver. You bring your own energy with you but it helps if you can draw energy from a source near by. That way we can continue the work until it is done. We do not need to breathe quite so frequently if there is an energy point near by.

Can we transmit energies that will reach out as batteries?

Oh yes! Anything left over from your meetings that you have not assimilated yourselves, or anything you have accumulated for what you require, you can ask for this to be collected and used for God's purpose with positive work.

Some people do transmission meditations.

There are many who do this kind of work for that specific reason. There are many groups, as you probably are aware,

---

[2] Bertrand Russell was an atheist

who are working on a slightly different vibration. Those vibrations are within another band. Think of telephone cables. They have many wires and many things that they use – these days I'm not familiar with their terminology – but within those bands there are many other bands, yes? Lines, if you like? Think of it as similar to that, the lines of communication.

NINE

Images and Conditioning

I'd like to talk for a little while about images and conditioning.

If you think of the word 'image' it is that which we present to one another is it not, in the outside world? We have our form as an image and we present a personality as an image. Behind that image is a great deal of conditioning, conditioning by your past lives. It is this conditioning which causes you a great deal of sorrow. It is by going through these different experiences brought about by conditioning that it is hopeful that you can learn what it is that you're not. If I said to you, or if I said to the medium, 'No, you must drop this image of being a good mother and leave your children', there would probably be a sharp intake of breath and a shocked feeling of 'I can't go along with that'. Others of you would have different conditionings. Now the image of a good mother, for instance, is that you do not leave your children or you do not do anything that would bring them harm. Now this does not mean to say that you should be anything in particular. It just simply means to drop the conditioning behind this and allow the true self to come through. While the true self functions you cannot do anything to harm anyone in any way. It would not be your purpose to harm anyone. It would simply be a state of being. Your true self would be operating through a physical body, but whilst we are in this dimension we cannot fully function perfectly, so there will always be some imperfections, even if you reach realisations to the fullest extent. But if your whole being is for the good and for love, your God-self would, of course, always take care of your child in one way or another, not necessarily by the image of yourself, for it may be necessary for the child to be looked after by God-Consciousness manifesting in another form or image, i.e. another loving human being.

This is very difficult to conceive at the ego level. On the ego level we individuate and feel total separation from one another.

I can present myself in any image or any form. I can present myself as the image of Julie or Brandon or Suzanne or Judy or Michael.' My image can be anything. Do you follow what I'm saying? If you take the sea water and put it in six different bottles would it be still the same water?

Yes.

Can you follow with this analogy?

If we knew who was talking to us it would help.

Do I have to be 'who'? I'm trying to talk to you about dropping the image and dropping your conditions, your conditioning! If you have a condition of being so terribly serious you will maintain a great deal of seriousness. If you can drop your conditioning there is a great deal of joy to be experienced. I'm just trying to take you one step further. This is a tiny step, but for you it may be a little difficult at this time but I'm giving it to you to think about. You may even be able to take it into your meditations whilst you are at home because only through experiencing it through yourself will you understand what I am saying. In a way you have to learn to know that which you are not, and then drop it. Peeling the onion, you'll be left with the essence.

It is hard for us to understand when you say you can present yourself as the image of each of us.

Yes, that's difficult to understand.

Coming back to the old analogy of a diamond, we are each a little part of the image of a diamond?

We can only see one part of it at a time, one facet at a time.

Would there be any truth if we said that we are you?

You're part of me. You just are, we just are, but we become one when we have dropped the images and the conditioning. We will each be an individual `I'. You will not lose your sense of being, but we will not be separate, we are not separate now. We are separated, in this dimension, everything is divided, or I should say it gives the impression of being separated and each is enclosed by their own darkness; the light is within but it is surrounded by the darkness of the conditioning and the images, and when that is dropped then each will know that they are part of the whole and that we are all one.

Yes. Would the term 'group soul' be applicable?

Yes, but even when we use the word 'group' it presents another image of division and even the word 'soul' should really be whole, to be the light. There are no edges to the light. Do you understand this? If there are two lights in a room you cannot say the end of one light is here and the end of the other light begins there. They merge together. This again is a very small limited analogy but perhaps you can follow it.

It does help, yes, it helps. When one has to get rid of the conditioning why do we have to have it in the first place? It serves a purpose presumably?

Does purpose not give you another image? In other words another set of conditions. You are seeking unconditional love, are you not? You are seeking to return to that. I will leave you now. It's a very small contribution. It just gives you a little something to think about, but bear in mind your thinking will have conditions on it so try to take it into your meditation and experience. We will help, we'll help. I give you my blessings. We are not far away, remember that. We do not spy on you, of course, we are only here at your invitation.

TEN

Childish or Child-like

I should like to speak of the difference between childishness and childlikeness. To be childlike does not mean to be childish. To be childish is to be as a child, not knowing how to behave in the mature world. To be childlike means to have an open mind and to be able to accept what surrounds you at any given time. To be childish is to respond negatively to criticism. To be childlike is to respond in an open fashion; by listening to voices from without you may be able to correct that which is not conducive to your thinking clearly. To clarify this a little more: if someone criticises you and you respond in a negative fashion, that is childishness. To respond with a childlike openness is to respond by seeing what it is you did wrong immediately, and with a wish to put it right. To be childlike does not mean you walk into danger without care and thought. That is what childish people do. They walk into danger and will not heed anyone else's warning and will do only that which they think is necessary.

To be childlike is to hear that voice within as well as the voice without. It is a little complicated, I do appreciate that.

It is very subtle, and to be able to tell the difference is going up one more step away from the obvious, the more obvious things like Thou Shalt Not Steal; fairly simple to you and me, but people who have very little when other people have a lot may consider that it is right to steal because someone is not distributing the wealth of the world correctly. In our society – I say ours because I was brought up in the same society as yourselves – most people have sufficient. I don't mean that they have everything that they want but most people on the whole have food and shelter. There are the few I must admit who have neither of these things but that is always going to be the case on the earth plane, I'm afraid, for a long time yet. Those are the more obvious things. The more subtle things are differentiated between the obvious and the not so obvious, to be led further in, to become aware of the reality of life, the reality of the spirit life, working through your physical life. It is difficult, if you are maturing yourself, to live with a childish person. It is even difficult to live with a childlike person if you are not of an open mind yourself, because a childlike person can often trigger off your own negative aspects. A childish person is difficult to live with because they will not give way. They will stick to what they want regardless of what you need, only seeing their own pathway, not seeing yours. Do you see what I mean? A very subtle difference.

Criticisms again strike at your self-esteem and this challenges your idea of yourself. It challenges your self-esteem and your pride is affected. Now there is no need to feel guilty about this. It is at least an awareness and you can sit quietly in your meditations and have a look and see what it is that is causing you the problem. If it is your pride, acknowledge it to yourself; you don't have to share it with anyone else except your inner God and the next time the situation arises, try to observe your reactions immediately, and in your next confrontation with anyone pray that you will be guided to react in the manner accordingly, in a childlike rather than in a childish way. It takes a great deal of discretion and discrimination, analysing and trust, because your emotional reactions are so quick that you find you are there before you know where you are and the situation has expanded into something you had no idea would occur. But when you try to go back over it you wonder how you got to this point, because the person reacts to you and you react to them and so it goes on in a defensive manner, but no-one really gets anywhere in understanding what the problem is, unless you have the childlikeness and the honesty to look within. This brings about a great deal of difficulty with people living together in families, and it is part of the problem of the marriages of people the whole world over. They come together, of course, for their karmic reasons, but with the difficulty in sustaining a partnership which is ultimately based on false values, it is a wonder that any of the marriages are sustained at all. To be able to promise to love 'till death do you part', for a start, is again an illusion. As you know, there is no such thing as death. So that is your first illusion. The second is, do you really know what love is when you make this promise? You may have an emotional attachment to someone, you may even form a dependency and you may get used to one another as a sort of habit, and you may temporarily be lifted beyond yourselves for a little while, but this does not necessarily make it a spiritual love that we all yearn for, and which we feel we should be able to understand. It is temporarily rather like one illusion living with another illusion, trying to expect reality to come to the fore.

If you are a childlike person and open in heart, and if you are very fortunate and have come through much karmic experience, you will find the love will grow between you because, instead, you promise to love the God within, with an understanding that there is no such thing as death. This has life within it, does it not? To bring the word 'death' into the marriage ceremony is rather incongruous, don't you think, with your knowledge of life eternal? When you think of it in those terms does it not seem a little odd? This again is learning to drop the conditioning. Whilst you have the conditioning it seems perfectly normal, does it not, to do this? To be able to walk side by side along the spiritual path together, supporting one another, this is very good and very helpful providing you both realise, what all you in the family realise, that your need for God is greater than your need for each other. But you can support each other through your difficult times with this in mind. Turn to God for what you need, do not expect if from another person. We all know how difficult it is to be perfect yourselves on the outside, yet we do expect the other person to be perfect for us, and to know all our needs at any given moment, and are greatly disappointed because they do not, and so we fall out of love with this person whom we thought was very Godlike in the original emotions.

Because you are of a mature age I have no doubt you have all experienced something of what I'm speaking about now. So I have a feeling that you understand what I am saying. You have an inkling, have you not, of the sorrow that can be caused by the loss of a dear one, but also loss of your dreams and your conditionings. It is painful to drop the conditioning; it is painful to see that that into which you have put your whole life has been based on an illusion. Now you have spent many years in a marriage with someone, only to find, and to accept, that the dream you had, that feeling that things were always going to be better between you, has not come to pass. Under these circumstances it is better to part, but part in a kindly manner and try to see that the other is not left sorrowing. It is difficult, for you cannot carry their soul for them; you have to let them go and follow your path on an inward spiritual search, and if it be on your own so be it. But again you see you're never totally alone, we can be with you. I understand you cannot all see us when we are with you, but I think you are all developing in the way to sense when someone is with you and I hope, with help from friends, that this can continue. Use whatever relationship you have with anyone as a friend or a marriage partner as a way to enlighten both of you so that you come into the next dimension ready to carry on. So it is not an end, it is a continuation of the spiral. Are there any questions?

We've noticed, in the Spiritualist Movement, a number of people changing partners and this is no doubt the reason, that the progression is not equal.

Yes, it becomes unbalanced and one person lets go of an attachment and the other one does not, and of course this is probably part of their karmic debt to one another, and it is very painful but sometimes very necessary.

I think we've been given a lot to think about.

There's a great deal of food for thought. I feel a little sadness around for some reason, I think in one of our friends who is not with us. I will be careful not to say too much here because I understand you do not want personal things on the tape. But just know that we are aware of the sadness and perhaps you can tell the person. We are linked up with some of you and we can feel your pain which unfortunately does affect the circle and the vibrations are a little lowered.

I think one thing that may be affecting us is not only personal matters but a feeling that the human race itself, on planet earth, is heading into difficult times. There does not seem to be anyone without trouble of some kind if you look around, and sometimes the heaviness can get you bogged down. I believe that there is a conjunction of planets at the moment which is causing a lot of upsets around a lot of people.

I am not au fait, as they say, with astrology, but many of my friends have told me this; those who have studied astrology and astronomy on another dimension. And this has a great deal to do with the different vibrations of each planet, because everything is a vibration and, even though they may be far away, they continue their vibrations and they affect you all the time, because your beings are all vibrating at different rates in your different bodies so it is bound to affect you. I am sorry it was a little sad today. We also feel the sadness, you know.

ELEVEN

Fear and the Process of Dying

The subject today is about the process of dying and the fear. As you probably know (or maybe you have not given it a great deal of thought), the moment you are conceived, all the time that the cells are being reproduced, there are also particles that are constantly changing which can be called, in your dimension, death. So in a way it would seem that from the moment that you are conceived you are in the process of dying. Herein again there are two illusions, one is the illusion of having just come into life and the other is the illusion of actual, so-called, death, because as you know you do not die; it is only your body that dies and in fact, simply changes form. So in a way you could say that from the point of conception you are continually changing form. Have you considered it at all in this way?

If you would like to take it into your meditation at some time you will perhaps have your own deeper realisation of what is actually happening. You become more aware of yourself as spirit through meditation because, as you know, you are spirit using the body, not the body using the spirit. The spirit comes first and the body follows a pattern that you have laid down from your innermost self, your innermost being. You have been provided with the body that you need at this particular time, in this particular incarnation. The type of body you have will determine, to a certain extent, the kind of experiences you have. For instance, if you formed yourself a very large body with heavy bones and enormous flesh, you would not, for instance, become a ballet dancer and you would not have the experiences of a ballet dancer and all that goes with that type of lifestyle. So you are given the type of body again, as I've just said, to be able to undergo the particular experiences you need to help you to unfold and become aware of different aspects of your being. And of course the karma that you have experienced in previous lives will most decidedly affect how you are going to be in the future. The type of thoughts you think are going to be connected to that body. Because of the type of thoughts your parents have had, what kind of people your parents were, that which your parents and grandparents have experienced, have all gone into the genetic make-up and been passed down to your body, so this body affects how you are in this life.

It's very difficult to comprehend. Your body has an intelligence of its own but it is all under the supervision of the spirit and the spirit part of you is the real you, you follow? The other intelligence is rather like a vehicle. You find out what you can do with these metals while you're on this planet and you shape them into different forms, yes? Again we're coming back to something of the copper. So in this way the different bodies are the different forms that can be made. We are basically, obviously, two arms, two legs, etc., but what a variation on a theme. Every person that is ever born is an absolutely individual person and has an individual type of body. You would know, would you not, that even if you were not living in your body and the medium was not in hers you would still be able to tell that you were not the other from simply looking at the bodies; the medium is not you and you are not the medium. Whereas at the moment I am wearing the body of the medium you know that it is not my body, it is hers, which I am borrowing at the moment so that I can express, just for a short time, a few of my views which have been gained from my experiences through many incarnations in the physical body and in other areas with a non-physical body. The physical body and your life here are just a minuscule part of the experiences you have had, and of the experiences that you are to have, but it is a very important part and it definitely affects how you unfold.

Now we come to the fear that goes with the idea of dying. Most people while on the earth plane try not to think too deeply about it, but of course it is presented to us on the television and in the newspapers. Even if you yourself never actually see a dead person you are constantly being informed that this is what in fact happens to human bodies. You see it sometimes with your pets, they have to pass on and you do in fact see the dead creatures. In the woods you may come across a dead bird, for instance, and it is through these little experiences children learn to understand that bodies are not a permanent thing. Of course you would not want them to be constantly surveying rows and rows of dead bodies, it would not be considered a healthy thing for a child to experience, but it goes a little way to help them to come to understand this, and that there is more life after death, that life always is, but in a different form.

Now when you have a near-death experience or if you have an experience where you have had to go into hospital and you have to contemplate the possibility of your demise, you're letting go of this most treasured possession. Even doing it temporarily under an anaesthetic is not something anyone really looks forward to. You have got used to your body, you're very attached to it, you'd say – excuse my little joke – but it is the attachment and the possibility of losing the body which creates the fear. Now the fear, to a certain extent, has its part to play. It helps you to stay in your body as long as you need to. So you take a little more care of it than you perhaps would otherwise. Now it is the attachment that causes the pain because if you've had to let go of anything – be it your car, your house, your possession, a dear friend – if you lose this possession you suffer; you suffer some pain of loss, you go through the grieving process, obviously depending on the value of the object to you, or the value of the person, because we do tend to regard our friends as objects many a time. We tend to forget their own individual personalities which have the freedom of spiritual choice in whatever limited form they have chosen. And again this is where the pain is caused by the attachment to the body of the person who is your beloved. First you have to remember that they are not an object to be possessed. You have to allow them the freedom to unfold and give them your love. Now, the next problem you might say to yourself is, well, how do I overcome this attachment? You overcome this attachment by going into your meditation and becoming aware of your spirit body. You become aware of your higher self so that you will know that you are spirit and that you are using the body. When this realisation comes to you, if you can practise your meditation in your quiet time, you will find that at the point of your death it will be an easy passing, you will just let go, though it is fearful before that time to face your fear. You may put it off, you may experience something in a small form in the night (that is when fear usually surfaces the most) because in your sleep you part with your body though you do stay attached by your cord, but we can help you to experience a little fear of death in a safe environment, knowing that through your meditations through your spirit body, and through your higher self you have made contact with us. If you can – through experience, through practice in your meditation, of going in the light, of trusting your helpers – if you dare to face this fear which is very real even though it is an illusion, you will experience the feeling as very real, but if you have got into the habit of tuning in to the highest within yourself regularly, then you will automatically go into that gear when you have faced this fear of death. Do you understand this?

It's like a lot of things we experience as humans. A lot of our life is lived through habits. We form habits very early on in life, some we would like to drop and cannot, or we think we cannot, but as we grow older we drop away childish habits and we learn to discriminate between the habits that can be beneficial and those which we must drop. The beneficial habits help us to live our lives more efficiently, to become habitual in thought and mind in the light and so organise our physical life accordingly. Again it is similar to riding a bicycle, once you learn to ride the bike you never really forget how, but if you have not practised for some time you may feel a little wobbly to start with. Now again, I repeat, if you practise your meditation and you become aware of spirit and have faced the fear of death beforehand, you will be able to slip gently out of this physical body and into the spirit world and recognise your friends and loved ones immediately. You will not go into that long deep dark sleep of forgetfulness. You will be able just to rest when you need and carry on with your work as you are doing now.

There's a lot of debate as to whether the near-death experience which people report is in fact like the process of dying. The psychologists are anxious to explain it as simply the dying throes of the brain and not a real contact with the spirit world. I don't know if you have any view on this?

This is where the scientists forget that they are already in contact with the spirit world. They think that they are coming into contact with the spirit world when they pass out of the body, but we are already, whilst in the body, in contact with the spirit world. The spirit world is everywhere and in everything. When they go through a near-death experience it is a recognition of this fact. If they had been meditating previously they would probably have recognised what was happening. It is partly the experience of the brain and reaction of the brain to the spirit coming out of the body, but they do not just begin to make contact with spirit after they've left the body. You follow this?

Yes, you're experiencing spirit all the time, so it's a combination. You cannot separate. The scientists tend to want to separate things and put them into little compartments. I had plenty of experience of this type of thought. It is very useful in certain aspects of the work but not when it comes to explaining infinity and spirit.

Two things here. Would it be right then that the brain, as the instrument of the mind, could possibly – when the spirit body is departing – carry on working for a while in a similar way to the body which actually continues to move for a while; the body's muscles contracting, etc? Does the brain actually go on working which might be part of the cause of this near-death?

There are these trace elements, yes, because people say you die suddenly, but of course you don't. As I've just said, you are dying from the moment you are conceived but it is only more obvious at certain points. It takes a little while for the body to die completely.

Fear and the Process of Dying

Perhaps the cells of the brain know they're going to die and maybe they're reacting against this. And secondly, something that was done thousands of years ago, by way of initiation – they would make somebody nearly die by putting them in a casket or under water and have a near-death experience so that they knew.

Yes, rather drastic! We're hoping that we don't have to do that here.

Would that have been intended in the same way as in meditation, to sort of practise dying; that it was practice of dying, but a very harsh one forced upon somebody?

Yes, you're correct.

A nurse once told me that after a doctor says the person has passed, if we continue to talk, the soul can still hear you talking at that moment.

Oh yes, yes.

That's the last thing that they hear, is that right?

Yes. They're probably standing next to you and listening to you talking. If they are conscious of actually coming out of the body they will understand. If not, they will wonder why you can't hear them.

That's usual, is it? As they just pass out of the body they are actually aware of it, they're not sleeping as they go out, they are aware of it?

Those who have been very ill, and perhaps in a coma, are not always aware, and older people tend to slip very easily from the body. But they, in a way, leave their bodies, practise leaving their bodies, in a more noticeable fashion. As you get older, become absent-minded, then you think in your mind that you're not all there. It's a feeling of not being completely in the body. It's a preparation for departing but it is quite varied; there's no hard and fast rule but the majority are aware of something. Children are the most easily aware.

You said, 'Go into meditation to try and find your inner self, your higher self'. How do you recognise that you've actually found it or reached it? I've tried it several times and I can't seem to.

I'm afraid the fact that you ask the question shows that you have not experienced your higher self yet. You will know. There will be no doubt. Persist. Do not believe the darkness you see; it is an illusion.

You spoke earlier of taking a drink of water to help you to keep contact, which interests me because I've been told from your side that water is the actual connection between the physical and spiritual, that the actual contact is made of water particles or the atoms of water and that's why our bodies are made of so much water.

Yes, and water can be in many forms, can it not? From being solid when frozen to being invisible when it becomes water vapour. It is a very fluid substance, very malleable, and there is water in the atmosphere all around you at the moment. Of course it is, as you said, within your bodies and you are exuding fluid all the time in the form of perspiration, and in other forms of a finer kind, and we can use the mind power that we have developed, both on the physical plane and in other dimensions, to mould ..... it's a little bit more complicated than this but you have the basis, yes?

Do you have to adjust your vibrations when you're trying to come in contact with a medium?

Yes, yes. We try not to make them too strong and so damage the nervous system. It takes quite some time to learn how to do it. You may observe that I am not moving around quite so violently as I have done in the past, I am learning to adjust my vibrations more to the vibrations of the medium, yes? It is all through the mind.[1]

We have to use what instruments are available. Perfection

---

[1] When Raynor first came through, Sheila's arms shook and the top part of her body swayed. This was pointed out to Raynor and, gradually, it stopped.

later. If we wait for total perfection I'm afraid no-one would come through very often anywhere. This is one of the difficult things I think people have, of accepting a medium's humanity. There is a tendency to expect perfection in all things if they are passing through spiritual teachings, but it is part of your process to learn to accept each other, warts and all, with love and understanding, as much as you would like other people to give to you. No, this is the joy of knowing your own failings but knowing that you are loved in spite of them and in that way you can share the love with all the others. It is a process of giving and taking.

TWELVE

Daily Development

How does one know whether one might be able to do mediumistic work?

It depends upon your desires, about whether you agreed to do this before you came and your seriousness with regard to your meditation. If you want to be able to impart some information to help your fellow beings, you are already doing that, are you not?

Can a medium accept what is coming through and be able to impart that? Maybe it's a case of time.

The medium probably needs to make the time, yes. You need to learn to trust and gain confidence and develop alone, yes? And this way of working is one step beyond what you are familiar with. Instead of passing the information from one to another we have been allowed to step into the vibrations of the medium and talk to you directly.

One of us will be joining a group for development, and the medium is coming as well. Would you do us the honour some time to come and teach us some of your philosophy? We will have half a dozen people there.

By all means.

Some different from the group you are now talking to.

Yes, I'll be one of many.

Well, you understand, it is not only myself, I am just the spokesman through the spokeswoman – do not forget her. There are many others and I just pass the information through that I have gleaned from many years of experience.

Do you have to digest the cacophony of instructions that come to you from members of your group?

But it is all given through the vibrations of love, so it is a form of ecstasy.

How do you decide about the subject you're going to choose on any particular day? Does it come upon you suddenly or are you prepared for this?

We are prepared, yes. We stay close with the medium – she does not always know this – but we stay close to the medium and depending on some of the experiences we have led her into, this helps to familiarise her with the subjects when we actually come to speak. We discuss it between us in the group; it follows in a certain sequence and sometimes we have to cover a little bit of that which has already gone before and introduce a little new thought along with it. It is the best way we have found, or I have found when I was teaching my pupils. It is best to repeat quite frequently what has been said before, but always going a little step onward, yes? So that the repetition helps it to go further into the mind and give a little bit more food for thought. So I personally tend to use this method but it is well prepared beforehand.

I feel your teachings are very valuable to us as a group but could also be valuable to a wider public.

We would be very appreciative if it could be passed on to

the wider public at some point. This would be our privilege because we realise it is very inspiring to hear uplifting sermons, but there comes a point when somebody wants to know .... well, how and when do I start and from where? And these little teachings are the where and the when and the how. Other people may be better at giving rousing speeches to inspire but I have found I am happier with this form.

You feel this is the bread and butter of instruction which sometimes is missed out?

That's right, yes, the bricks and the mortar; we help to provide a good foundation, we hope. There's no point in rushing too far ahead in wanting to save the world and convert humanity if you haven't learnt to lift yourself. Humans have a tendency to topple off their pedestals if they jump on to them too quickly. So it is best to build a good foundation and go at a steady pace, we have found.

You've seen a few topple off their pedestals?

If they go far too fast, they then come into contact with more temptations and if they have not developed strength previously they can fall and put themselves back two or three lives, which is very sad.

Do you have any numerical idea as to how many lives you have reincarnated?

I am afraid that is beyond me. I am sorry. It is so many, but of course in a strange way while you're experiencing your life on earth in a physical body you are also experiencing life in spirit. At the beginning of the talk I mentioned that you are constantly in spirit so you are living life on several levels at any given time.

Our consciousness tends to be restricted in this life?

Yes, and then when you pass into sleep, again you are experiencing life in another dimension. So things do not always develop in exactly the same moment. If you think of a graph there are different lessons and you have different levels depending on which body you're having experiences in at the time. You have your physical, and your emotional, and your spiritual, and all these have to be moulded to become as one. Do you follow me? It's almost as though, while all these graphs are at different levels, there are all these gaps at the top. A rather silly analogy, I'm afraid, but you are learning to experience becoming whole. You are already whole in spirit but you just don't know it yet.

So the different levels have got to catch up with each other, is that the idea?

Something like that. You see, you may find someone who is very emotionally well balanced but mentally they're a little short on wisdom, or vice versa. You may sometimes be very practical on the earth plane but totally dead spiritually in the conscious mind. I don't mean they're not spirit, it just means not in their conscious mind. You have to have the love and the wisdom. They are two of the pillars towards becoming conscious of spirit and love, unconditional love.

But this balancing doesn't necessarily have to happen in one physical life?

No, that is true. But having to come into a physical body it just seems to take a long time.

The thing I find hard to understand is the higher self – the one that's really doing the progressing – using the lower self for little experiences. Therefore is the higher self in fact in need of these experiences to perfect itself?

Your higher self does not need to perfect itself.

So why does it allow the lower self to go through all this?

Freedom of choice.[1]

---

[1] The lower self is made up of illusions and conditioning from past lives.

How would an ordinary person know whether we're getting there, getting it right? Is there any clue?

On the odd moments when you feel a great deal of love and joy and also the amount of difficult situations you find yourself in. If life is going along too peacefully you may have slid into a backwater. So if a great deal of things happen around you and your lessons are popping up all over the place you will know that you are on your way. If you are sitting smugly back in your armchair thinking I don't have to do any more, I'm O.K. Jack, then you're not going anywhere.

Many times I used to wish I could sit back in my armchair and think, `I'm all right, I have arrived', but unfortunately each time I did that I went out of the door and fell over. Pride comes before a fall, very true.

A little bit like Richard Bach saying that if you're still alive you haven't fulfilled your purpose yet.

I feel more relaxed this afternoon in spite of the medium's rushing around.[2] I think we are becoming more efficient and I do take notice of what you say about any movements and of course we need to perfect this form of communication and we are aware of your contribution. This could not be done without your willing help and without your love and acceptance because if there is too much of a negative element in any group it forms a resistance. It is not impossible; it just makes things harder for us to come through.

---

[2] I had to rush from the school, where I was dealing with about a hundred children at lunch-time, to the home where the meetings started at 3 pm. Raynor is referring to being told about the shaking of my arms and body. This never bothered me but the others were afraid it might hurt me in some way.

THIRTEEN

Love

The subject today is love and everything in relation to it. We use the word 'love' in English to symbolise a vast subject, but I will only be able to touch on it a little bit this afternoon. The word love, just as a code, is of a certain vibration, but unconditional love at the very highest level is actually the pure energy of God, and it is from this energy and from that level that everything else emanates. But from our dimension, and from yours, we all experience it at various levels at different intensities in varying degrees.

Now in the body it can be experienced in the lower chakra as a sexual energy for creating; through the mid-centres you can feel the energies at the different levels of the chakras appertaining to the different bodies, around and interpenetrating your physical body. It is felt in the heart centre as love for one another, or love for everything else, but of course while it is still on a human level it brings attachments with it that cause us the pain. It isn't the love that causes the pain, it is the attachments which we form. Levels of energies pass out from you to whatever object or whatever person takes your interest, or to anything that you feel on the emotional level. These threads come out from you, from different chakras again, so that you are joined in various ways. We will talk first of people. You are joined to these other people at the different levels of your chakras. Do you follow this? It is as though threads of light come from the different chakras to the other person and join up with their chakras on the same levels. So you could say that you were linking up your different bodies together so that when you withdraw from one another, when you part, you are not necessarily parting. If you're parting on the physical you can still be joined on the other levels, you understand, so long as the love and the relationship and the closeness can stay together, even though you're physically parted.

But, on the other hand, you could be living together and not be linked together at some of the other deeper levels or higher levels. You may be joined here on the physical through habit, through necessity, but you may not be joined in any other chakras and you can feel very much alone even though you're living with another person. You can be parted from somebody you love but you can still feel very close. It is because you are linked on these other levels; you are still in touch with one another. So you can be at the other side of the world and still feel close and still feel that link. You can be passed from this dimension, the earth plane, to other dimensions and you can still feel close so long as the love link is there. Now when you part through progression, or through misunderstandings, it is partly because you are not linked on the other levels. You may not be linked on the mind level, therefore you will not see eye to eye, but you could still be linked on an emotional level, so that despite the fact you don't see eye to eye you're still bound together through your emotions. There will be a lot of quarrelling, a lot of arguing, but this other emotional level will keep you together for as long as you continue in your illusion that you're in love. Because on the lower emotional level if it doesn't have any of the higher, it is purely a playing together of the two emotional bodies, a constant movement; the relationship will not be based on wisdom or knowledge. Do you follow?

If you are linked on your spiritual levels you can spend your life living at the opposite sides of the earth but still be linked, and if you have been progressing on your spiritual path you will be aware of this link. You'll also be aware that you have cut away, or drawn back into your body, these other threads to do with the lower levels, so that you can continue your life on the planet without the need for the other's physical presence. You understand this? Now when your relationships break and you feel the pain you can actually feel as though you're bleeding. I don't know if any of you have experienced this sensation? You know you mostly feel the pain in the heart centre and in the solar plexus. That's because the threads have been torn apart and they are hanging loose still; they have not been withdrawn back into the body. So in a way some of your energy is still passing through but not going anywhere except that it has been dispersed into the general atmosphere. Thus it gives you the feeling that you are losing energy or, as some people will express it, they feel as though they're bleeding inside, or they feel as though they're falling apart. You could withdraw the threads back into the body much quicker if you have been meditating and learning these things. If you're not very stable, if you're not very developed, it may take many years, and it possibly can even take several lifetimes, to really heal and be withdrawn back in so that it doesn't leave a scar.

Because – again in the same way that you have a wound in your physical body – it leaves a scar with scar tissue which can sometimes be very knotty and be very painful. In the same way this can happen in your etheric body; you can leave a scar of energies incompletely healed, because if it was healed completely the scar would be removed. If you had been going for healing, for instance, the healers from our side could smooth away the collection of energy in your etheric body. This knots together; it seems to form a kind of a knot. And the healers can smooth it away so that the person can be healed. This is how you can help if you are doing healing.

Now as to the love energy in relation to sexual relationships. Unfortunately the Christian church has taught that it is sinful, so unfortunately many, many people are still carrying this sentence of guilt that they've enjoyed sex or that they feel sexual. It is almost as though this is the dark side of the moon. It is something that had to be put up with in the past to procreate and to continue the development of human bodies instead of seeing this energy as part of the God-power and special. The Christian church has tended to make women in particular feel as though they are second-class citizens and men have gone along with this, and then the women collude with this idea because they go on to teach their children the same thing, even though within themselves they don't feel good about it. Fortunately it is not so prevalent now. Even the people in the churches are a little bit freer in their thinking and, of course, it has gone somewhat overboard like anything else that has suddenly been released. It is an energy that has been well suppressed in the Christian lands and it has burst out. Like anything else it will eventually balance itself out individually. This energy is the God energy felt in the lower chakras.

Now if young people just come together without having

matured and come together too soon without learning to control anything about themselves, either their mind, their emotions or their bodies, they will be in a constant state of flux, they will not be able to make stable relationships because they have not been taught a great deal about self-control. It's all to do with competition, competing against one another. Now you would think that this would bring a certain amount of control, but it is only certain cautions that are brought into the self-control, and it is for selfish purposes; it is all to do with themselves. They're not encouraged to include the other; it is always that you must win for yourself, not for the benefit of others. It is perhaps temporarily given to them, as in winning for the school, but it is on a lower selfish level. It is, again, competitive against another school; it does not include the benefit of the other school. That is part of our way of life. Now if only young people could be taught more about their different bodies, for they only know about their physical bodies, their feelings and what they think, but they don't know why or where it comes from. Because they know nothing of their past lives, it is as though they have no roots whatsoever. It is rather like a plant trying to grow without any roots. They do not have anything to draw on for their spiritual progress. Obviously, they progress to a certain extent as even plants do. They limp along through life without any knowledge of how to tune in to God because they don't know about God and most of them would laugh anyway. This again is very sad. But on the other hand there is no need to push God down their throats.

All that really needs to be done is to help them to be aware of everything else and that everything else should be treated, as they would like to be treated, with care. They are great followers; they will mimic what you do. So if the majority of older people are careless and non-thinking, non-aware, then unfortunately the majority of young people will be the same. They are like sponges; they absorb what is around them and if they are not brought up in a loving atmosphere, then unfortunately they see that their parents are not in control of situations, nor of their emotions nor their minds, and have no use for the spiritual at all.

So you can see what a state the planet has come to. This does not mean that the spirit is not working. Of course it is. You cannot escape from spirit, everything is made up of it, but it is not in the conscious mind; it has not made that link to the higher chakras. Fortunately there are a few old souls still coming here and of course they have an awareness deep within. They do not feel that they are in the right slot, so to speak; they feel a bit like a square peg in a round hole. They rebel and they're the youngsters who tend to get into a lot of trouble. They are seeking, they are not just accepting what is happening around them and unfortunately, because they're different, society will jump on them. They are the demonstrations of the fire, the energy, the heat, the fuel, sending out sparks. Does this sound familiar?

If you can tune into your higher selves you will know, my friends, when you experience that sense of purity, absolute cleanliness, that which is of a finer substance. But of course you need to build all your other levels as well so that your other bodies can cope with the God energies at a higher level without burning out your nervous system, and when all these bodies are balanced you begin to feel as though you are in touch with the whole of everything. You then become aware that you are a whole person and you have no need to fear anything because you are part of the whole. You know that your home is not here and that, although they may destroy your body, they cannot destroy you. That takes away the fear. And of course nobody else can actually give it to you, it is yours for the asking but you have to do the work beforehand and it will be God's grace and God's gift in God's time but you must knock, you must ask. Would you like to ask me any questions?

Yes, please. You said old souls; does this imply the continuous creation of souls?

I'm told that it is a terminology used for people who have been coming to the earth planet for some time. I am told creation is a continual absolute now. I cannot give you any further descriptions that would really help you in your sense. So there is no past and no future; there is only the now, so there is always continual creation of being.

Continuous generation.

So when you get to those levels the terminology of old or new is not relevant, but it is used in relation to those who draw close to the material or have been on the material planet for aeons of time, because there are those who do not come this far down.

Could you tell us about the subtle bodies? I'm always a bit confused as to the chakras and the names of the bodies.

There is usually confusion in the terminology depending on which philosophy or way of life you choose, and even in this particular philosophy the terminologies or names used for the different bodies can be confusing, but I will use the words, the physical body, the etheric body, the astral body, the mental body and the spiritual body.

Is one of these the emotional body?

The astral body is the emotional body. It is in relation to the heart chakra. The etheric body is linked closest to the physical. It's all to do with your sense of security – your home, your physical home – and that's why, when you are threatened, when your physical body is threatened or you are threatened with the loss of your physical home, this is where you feel it. It is the body closest to your physical body. Can you follow? Of course any threat to your emotional body is here (indicates the solar plexus). Any threat to your thinking processes and how you express yourself is here. And at this area – which causes your link with your higher levels (indicating the brow) – there are several chakras within and very close together. They are not always those that are shown when people are teaching; they just give you the main ones. There are many in your hands and your limbs and in other parts of the body, but those mentioned are just the main ones. And there are some who may put it slightly differently but in general I think we can take other people's teaching and fit it in with what I've just said.

Are the mental body and the spiritual body two different things or are they the same?

No, they are two different things.

You were referring to young men who are against the system, who rebel and don't want to conform. Did you mean that they are old souls?

Yes, yes. They have a feeling within that what they are being taught is not the absolute, that there are other ways of doing things and other ways of looking at things.

Yes, but why do they create so much havoc at times?

It's the energy, the God energy within, when it moves. It is difficult if the other bodies are not stable; it tends to send them off in different directions. They have not had a good grounding in self-control, or a stable background, or you'll find they've not been able to build up stable other bodies.

So should one try to control them or should one leave them to go in many different directions in the way they do?

It is really teaching them self-control, but you have to be very much in control yourself. If you wish to try and control them you have to be very firmly in control of yourself before you should even attempt it, because they will manipulate you. They're often quite powerful souls and they will manipulate you. Through the energies, and if you have not got self-control yourself, they will manipulate you and cause more havoc. So first you must have self-control and then try to teach them about self-control, which is not easy. And of course if you're demonstrating it they will fight against you but they will have more respect for you. They will not admit it at first but it will come; they will have a growing sense of respect if they know that they cannot manipulate you whichever way they want. And then, just put them in the light and radiate love in their direction. I know it is not easy to give a demonstration of affection to someone who is manipulating you left, right, and centre, and perhaps always arguing and rebelling against you. So the best way then, when you have your quiet time, is to radiate as much love as you can towards them and put them in the light and ask for their protection and then to trust God. It is a lesson in trust. When I say that the other body is totally separate it is just for our discussion. Of course nothing is totally separate. As you understand, it is all merging, but you understand what I mean, I think.

Is it all part of a continuum, the different bodies and the whole range of life?

Yes, everything merges on the other level. It is only on the physical level that everything is separate, or seems separate. This is part of the problem with the sexual energies. You are drawn together, you feel you want to merge and of course you cannot because of your physical bodies. They do not merge, but you can have a temporary merging of your other bodies, and this is where there is a deep spiritual love for one another and you are merging together on all the other levels as well. This is where you get the sense of oneness and where the idea of being married and living as one comes from. The benefits of the one should always include the other, but of course the survival of the ego does not always include the survival of another ego, so there we have a conflict on the physical levels. It is not easy even if you're merging on the spiritual level because the energies, of course, come down through the different bodies and if you have not developed the self-control then there are more powerful energies being played with and more damage can be caused.

My friends have taught me that physical love originally is to draw people together so that they begin to learn about love; that it is used so that people begin to love back. The original is not for the sake of love but merely for a continuation of species. I always try to say that love is the same thing whether it's being expressed physically or at a very high level; it's merely the covering that is being used that changes it. But the love is the same and that love is the God energy, all the way through, and that doesn't change. Some people seem to think there are different qualities of love.

Yes, it's rather like the essence of the onion, isn't it? You can remove the onion but you're still left with the essence. That would be the pure love. The other coverings are rather like the coverings on the onion and that is what distorts the purity. It's rather like looking through one of those mirrors that distorts everything.

But not to decry any sort of love, because somewhere at the bottom, although covered over, it is, as you say, the God energy and we're learning and moving towards it through these things.

Yes, it will move you into situations whereby you will rub up against someone else and, if you're alert, you will be able to use each situation for learning. Everyone is your teacher because the God-life is in everyone. The person who is irritating you the most at any given time can be your teacher of the moment, for which one should give thanks! One doesn't feel inclined to, but you can do it later. Yes?

Yes. People say, you know, 'Oh, but it's only a physical love, it's not the real thing', but it is the real thing. All love is the real thing. It's only what you're making of it and how you're expressing it that might be a bit lower.

They may have only come to the point where they love themselves in a selfish way. It is partly to do with the survival of the physical; if it is not expanded to include more than self-love, then you could say it's of a lower nature but it is a covering, yes?

I find some people, who are supposedly well on the path, express it that way but I don't think I can agree with them.

It is because they live in a world where everything is separate and they are simply expressing the way they see it. If you feel unhappy and depressed, and low and angry, then the world becomes a lonely, depressing, angry place, and everything in the world is angry and depressing. If you are a loving person you live in a different world, even though you are on the same physical planet and, of course, by the type of thoughts you give out you draw the situations to yourself accordingly. So if you're giving out a lot of hatred and a lot of anger, people should not be surprised if the same sort of things come back. Unfortunately, or fortunately – it depends how you look at it – the God-energy can stir other people. If you have got to the point where you're radiating more light than most, if you go into other areas where people are not quite so spiritually developed, the energy within yourself will either draw people to you, or the God within themselves will attract them to you, and those who don't want to look into the light will run away or may want to fight with you.

I was going to say, 'Get angry with you'.

They will want to use you to prove it, because they do not realise that they have to prove it for themselves and they have not yet learnt to read the maps. In other words, they have not read the books or discussed it on deeper levels. They still have this idea of superiority and inferiority, and this continual to-ing and fro-ing or seesawing which affects them emotionally and mentally.

I have seen their previous lives joining people. It interests me that you might be joined on a higher level but not on lower levels. Do you think that might happen if you meet somebody and you feel something for them but they don't return it? On a physical level they haven't realised it but on a higher level that's what has been recognised.

That's right, yes.

Perception.

They are, of course, joined but they are not conscious of it.

You did say that the young people who have no knowledge of their previous lives are like a plant without a root?

Of course it was a very general statement.

I think it's true for many of us. Would you advocate the practice of things like psycho-expansion where people try to find out about their previous lives, in that case?

If people do search out their past lives they must realise they have to be responsible for knowing. They will no longer be able to say, 'But I did not know that'. They have seen. Therefore, there is more risk in receiving information into your conscious mind; then they are more responsible for what they do afterwards. As a child you get a certain amount of leeway or allowances made. Even yourself, when you're rearing a child, you make allowances for the child's behaviour, but once the child knows and then deliberately disobeys you, you take the matter more seriously, do you not? It is the same.

Can some threads be fairly immediate in that you put them out and then withdraw again?

Yes, every little thread can be sent out and withdrawn. It

is the same process as when you're shopping. You see things and you send the thought out. Now if you continue to feed the thread by thinking about the object which you have the intention of buying, your thought stays with it, but if you're sending your thoughts up to a higher level this is the process you can use to link in with the higher levels, to help you lift. You could say you're almost helping to pick yourself up by your bootlaces.

So that's why it's good to do it in a group because you can all help each other?

That's right, you learn to resonate. The old story of the tuning forks, yes? One can resonate another and if you're all learning, reading and studying and discussing, one who is pushing ahead more energetically than another will actually help the others unknown to them. They are all part of the whole. They just have different ways of putting things.

How long can it take when someone has had some sort of a break, unfortunate break, either death or divorce or something like that, for them to break and assimilate the threads so that they feel whole again?

It can take three years, but of course if they've got a lot of help, it can help them to cut the time down. If they are meditating it will ease, but there is a degrading process through either divorce or through death or the loss of anything.

I suppose they can lengthen it and not let it heal?

Yes, if they continue to persist in the 'Why me?' Again, it's rather like an octopus's tentacles, they can almost hug the pain to them. It's almost as though they are hanging on to this bottle of poison, complaining every time somebody tries to take it away from them. They have become attached to it, so this thought goes round and round in their heads instead of their recognising that this is what they're doing. They can ask for help. If they repeat, 'I can't cope' over and over again during the day, is it surprising that this person does not cope? Or any other negative thought, where they are using the energy in a negative fashion.

People who teach counselling have done a lot of work now on looking at it from this side only. It would be so useful if they knew of the other side as well.

All you can do is just persist in doing that.

To what extent are our lives pre-determined?

They're pre-determined by your past karma.

You mean that I pre-determine?

You have in that sense the same amount of freedom as a donkey on a chain, until you begin to see through the illusion. You have the amount of freedom within the limits of your karma that has gone on before. It is how you face all these experiences which determines your amount of freedom. The freedom on the earth plane is a total illusion; you're never, ever going to have total freedom on the physical plane because the only way you have total freedom is to be there on your own, and you're never going to be on the earth plane on your own, because the minute you're on your own without a sense of God you are lonely. So you will seek for someone else to join you in your life and then you have to take into consideration their needs. You tend to see freedom perhaps as, 'I want to do what I want – whenever'. Now the only freedom, the real freedom, is to be aware of the God energy, the love, the unconditional love, so that is what you emanate, you are that. You're not just thinking it, you become it, it is you. You are actually that but it is not in your conscious mind. If you are emanating this unconditional energy all the time you are no longer manipulated by other people's problems; you do not respond. If they are coming at you with a particular ego problem, because you do not have that ego problem in you, you do not respond, you just emanate unconditional love. You are free, and all the energies of the planet and of the other levels are there for your assistance in the work that you are doing here because, for anyone who has come to that state of realisation, the ultimate state of unconditional love is only to help others. A realised being just lives and is in that state of being. He does not think and express himself intellectually; he just expresses unconditional love at all times through what he says and what he thinks and what he does. It is a little difficult to comprehend unless you've seen these other energies.

Thank you for your help. We do realise that we could not work in this way without it and we do realise a lot of the other work that goes on, and I have been asked to pass on everyone's thanks for your work. There have been five golden rings around the circle today on the different levels from the different chakras.

FOURTEEN

Aspects of Infinity

It may come as a surprise for you to be reminded that you are in fact aspects of the infinite. You already exist in the infinite. You are part of the energy of the infinite and the information that you glean through your souls and minds is fed back to the creator and each of you has an individual perspective on your experiences. Each one is totally individual in your experience, your different ways of handling experiences, your emotions and the way you use your mind. All is fed back into the ultimate energy, but it passes through other levels of energies or other dimensions, whichever way you like to put it. Now you may say why is this necessary? This thought-world on the mental level is a source of energy for other aspects of the infinite to use. For those who do not wish to come this far down into the physical, this information and energy is fed to the appropriate dimension on the mental and emotional levels to those who are operating mainly on that vibration.

You remember my speaking to you about the connection through the chakras, to each other and to different levels? Well, this is another branch of what we were discussing the last time we were together. This links you with other levels of vibration and you operate on these levels in other times. I'm suggesting the word 'time' because we do not have many words that we can use to convey to you other moments in the infinite between the spaces. That which takes a long time here can happen in a twinkling of an eye on another level and even less than a twinkling of an eye on a higher level. So you can actually be living in these different dimensions all at the same time. We do really mean something different from what you experience here. In a way you can use the analogies of the aeroplane travelling through the air and the cars travelling on the land and the boats travelling on the water. They all travel at different speeds because they have different problems to contend with, other aspects of your planet. Each vehicle that you use has to deal with some particular physical aspect and of course it is somewhat different on the land and the water and the air. You follow this?

It's a very rough analogy, I'm afraid. So, in a way, the different bodies that you use on these other levels have different energies which you need to learn to deal with. So you are experiencing life at different levels and you are learning to control the energies and to assimilate the information that you receive, first from yourself, and from other people, in a similar way that you can discuss with each other here. You can hear about somebody's problem, you can hear how they deal with it and you can apply it sometimes to your own life. You can either decide, 'That's not the way I'm going to deal with my problem', or you can think, 'Well, that has helped me, I will have a look to see if I can help someone else'. Again, this is happening in varied forms on other levels. You are living in another dimension, so you learn to deal with the energies. And all those energies are brought into play or collected by other people's thoughts and passed through into other finer dimensions. This will be a little difficult to grasp because you perhaps do not bring back too much in your memory or conscious mind of your existence at other levels just yet, but you may find that it feels familiar, when you think about it, and possibly feasible. Do give it some serious thought; it's very feasible but it may seem very strange to you because maybe you have not considered this possibility before.

Now when you pass from your physical body at death you go on the other side for some time to whatever level you have attained. You may decide to live on that level for a little while or you may decide you want to rest. You may decide that you want to carry on learning or you may wish to come back to the planet and help, as do other aspects of the infinite. You can sit and rest if you like, but I think when you discover what energies you have, you will be only too happy to join in with the light and love of the infinite. There are many lower aspects as well, beings who work on the lower vibrations. They have their place in the scheme of things and they're also learning, but you are now drawing away from things like that and are coming more into relation with the light, and this is what you have come here for. Your purpose is to learn to live in the light whilst in the physical body and to bring it into your physical bodies and keep it in your conscious minds, and know that wherever you go you are taking that light with you. You follow?

This is not just thinking about it now and again. Obviously if you concentrate in meditation you go deep into it; this helps, but it is having it here in the back of your conscious mind all the time, the responsibility that you have taken upon yourselves because it is a personal responsibility. Even though we live in a unity we are allowed to accept this responsibility and use it. This ability to respond is a responsibility; you have a response, you give a response to the call from the light. You are responding to that call which is you. It is a difficult aspect to grasp; here you are, separate individuals, yet all living on one planet, are we not? So in one way or the other we are really all in contact with the earth. Even if it is by sitting in a chair which is in touch with the ground which is in touch with the earth. In our physical bodies we are part of one planet. Our physical bodies are made up of the substances of the physical planet so that makes us one unit. So we are not as separate as we tend to think of ourselves in the physical body.

On the other levels where you are more aware of this unity, there is not the same division, and it is coming into your conscious mind that this unity goes on into ever widening dimensions. I say widening because when you come from the darker domain you always feel as though you're lifting and expanding. Your knowledge and your sense of love, and your awareness of light and freedom, always expand to the level in which you can vibrate in comfort. You can temporarily pass into the next domain in company – I think I've mentioned this before – so that you may experience a little of that dimension to help you to lift and desire to move on. But it is not like physical desire. It is not something that is out of your control. It is a call from the Infinite Being and it is your response to that call which draws you on. And one thing you have to realise whilst you are still on the planet is that as you become more powerful in your mind you are becoming more in control of your life. So that what comes to you, you have called to yourself. I am afraid you cannot any longer sit back and say, 'Why has it happened to me?' You have to accept this responsibility. You have drawn it to you so that you may learn how to deal with the energies and how to carry these energies to other beings to help them to vibrate at a slightly higher rate than they do already. So wherever you go, whatever you touch, you are leaving energy behind. You have only to think of psychometry; every stone carries its history within its vibrations, every article. So just imagine; your vibrations are much higher than the stones, just imagine the energy that you are leaving behind. Wherever you go, this is a responsibility, is it not?

We use the expression a lot, 'into the light'. Are we talking about physical light, photons, etc?

Again the photon vibrates at a very high rate, yes? And you call it a photon in this dimension, but in our dimension we feel it as love and see it as light, but of course the light vibrates at a much higher rate the higher you go. So you can give them different names but it still does not really explain what they are. It would not help you. It is difficult. Let me see if I can get a picture that will help to explain it. I'm getting the picture of a heavy substance being dropped into another substance. Now the stone into the water causes the ripples. The stone and the water are of this planet but they're different vibrations, one is more subtle than the other. And so, on the other dimensions within each band, you get a variety of vibrations. Some more subtle than others, yes? And so on and so forth.

Giving names would not really help but each particle, each vibration, each particle of light is like a hologram. It is rather like each raindrop which can reflect the sunlight but it does not carry sun in it, it just carries the reflections and the vibrations of the water and the vibrations of the light around it. I suggest you think on that quietly when you're in your meditation and we will try to convey to you, through thought, when you are on your own. In fact if anyone else would like to consider this we may be able to convey it best to you that way rather than through words. Do we have any more of your questions?

Yes. Some of our scientists talk about tachyons which go at a speed faster than light. Do you have any views about this?

Thought is even faster than light.

Could it be instantaneous?

Thought is nearest to being instantaneous, more than the light, yes, because through thought we can travel to different parts of our particular domain and those below at any given moment; we can, through thought, be wherever necessary. So you could say that we are faster than the things that the scientists are discovering, but I do understand that they are beginning to be aware that there are things beyond the physical of their dimension. However I think they are somewhat suspicious because they have logical minds and this does not fit in with their logic. But those who are developing their intuition are able to pick up on the information that some of the scientists on our side are conveying to them, and are trying to prove their theories. The theory comes first and then it is followed through by trying to discover whether it does in fact work on the physical planet. But of course they will have some problems because, as I say, the logical mind has to be very suspicious all the time and they do find it very difficult to relax and listen to their intuitive sides.

It seems a shame that; they're missing out on so much more.

Well again this is the problem that they have given themselves, and they have come to manage the energies and they have to be aware of the limitations of the logical mind.

The thoughts you say travel fast and so they are somewhere; I understand they go somewhere. Is this haphazard?

Nothing is haphazard, no. We use the expression 'going somewhere' because on the physical plane there is always somewhere to go. The physical plane is surrounded and intermingled with the energies. The finer energies fit into the spaces between the dense vibrations; there are wider spaces for the finer energies to interpenetrate. You could say that the spaces between the earth, the moon and the sun are rather like the atoms and the molecules. So there is a great deal of space in between the moon, the sun and the earth. If you were in your body as a tiny microscopic being there would be a great deal of space between your energies for these other tiny energies to move through. We're getting very technical today, are we not?

I gather that sense of humour continues into these other dimensions. Is that right?

Oh, thank God there is a sense of humour! We try not to take everything too seriously because humour is to do with joy and love.

So when you say that our thoughts are high somewhere, they're high somewhere as energy? Is that what you're saying?

Yes.

But at different levels?

And they can take the shape of form. That is why certain people can project their image and others can see the form, depending on what level and how intuitive they are. This is how we travel through the vibrations if you like. We project an image of our form. In a way, you could almost say that I wasn't really here because my source of thought is not on your level of vibration. I am projecting a thought form of myself to your level, and it operates from where I am which is not so much in a different place but in a different level.

When you passed over, did you find that you were an aspect of a larger being?

We all tend to form groups which are all part of ourselves – our greater self – and those greater selves form other groups which are part of another greater self, and so it goes on in intermingling groups. In a similar way you are all part of this group and some of you are part of other groups; you are also part of family groups; you are also part of work groups and so on.

As we are today, have we ever met in a previous existence?

You mean yourself and myself or the whole group?

Well, anyone here, have we been together before?

We are all part of our higher self but we have not always met whilst in the physical body. We may have been incarnated at different times. Some of us help from the other side while others incarnate. You understand? So we have met on other dimensions, but not always in the physical, and on the higher levels we are all part of one anyway.

Coming through a circle in Devon organised by the White Brotherhood a large number of people of various statuses came through to describe their life, their death and their passing. I have always thought these to be genuine. We have had people who were, when they were on earth, Pandit Nehru, Indira Gandhi and George VI, but many more ordinary people, and one or two people have suggested that this is an illusion, that these are not genuine transmissions and I've been rather concerned recently to know before I go on again, as to how genuine these are. I think they're genuine.

Yes, they're all part of the brotherhood and sisterhood of light. Those who think other people are illusions are suffering from illusions themselves and that is probably the problem that they have to deal with whilst upon the earth planet: to learn the difference between reality and illusion. In one sense all our lower aspects of the infinite are somewhat of an illusion; if you take it that far, anything that takes the form is an illusion, but in the sense that you will need, they are genuine.

In a sense everything except God is an illusion, is it not?

That's true. It is not an easy thing for egos to consider. No-one likes to think that they are an illusion, and the pain and suffering you feel is very real but it is not from your real self; it is the aspect of the personality that you are using at any given time. The real self is the God and love energy that is within each personality and which the personality is masking. They're covering up their light with many non-realities.

Thank you. I was very interested in your remarks where you said that we should try to lose our conditioning by throwing overboard all the different previous ideas. Should I throw over my ideas that I'm listening to you and that these people are here? I don't know how far to go!

Well, no matter how far you go you'll still be living in your illusion for the time being, of being in a physical body! So you can play the game. You will know when you've hit the right spot.

We'll play it within reason. I suppose I need the illusion to keep going?

Well, just temporarily. I don't know about the need ..... but you have it whether you like it or not, at present.

I have this illusion that I'm sitting here in somebody else's body talking to you and I shall have to ask my friend if I'm really doing it! Or are you all figments of my imagination?

Or are we all just thought-forms going through your head?

Ah yes, you see, you are all thought-forms.

You've got your eyes shut. Can you see us?

I see your energies.

And yet sometimes at a Spiritualist church they'll come through and say, 'She's wearing my ring'. Is that just an energy form?

It is an energy form, yes. We have to learn to recognise what we see, and interpret the energies that we see, and from those of us who have had lives on the earth plane, of course we do not forget what these things look like. Those beings who perhaps have not experienced much life on the earth plane may need to learn a little more from us. They have lessons of course if they wish to have some experience. Some people like to draw close and just observe. They don't want to be particularly helpful; they don't want to be involved; they just want to observe.

Have any members of your group been in fact on other planets and not this one?

Some of the higher members of the group of our higher self – we would call them perhaps teachers or avatars – are able to travel further than the physical dimension and they are able to communicate with their brothers on the other planes or other planets. I'm able to receive information through thought-forms of life on other planets but I have chosen to work closer to the earth plane for the time being.

I am told by scientists that there can be no life on many planets because human beings could not exist there but can these subtle bodies live on these other planets?

Yes, they live within the energies of any particular planet necessary for their spiritual evolvement, or their managing of energies, or having the experiences.

Why is there suffering as well as joy? Couldn't we all have been created happy?

It is God learning and growing, God the creator, God the created and God the creating energy. I think in the churches they call it the Trinity but I do not think they understand what it really means.

A teacher from Cyprus said, 'You are all Gods in the making. Will you then be lazy Gods?'

That is a thought! In a way you are little Gods in your own home, are you not? You have sway over what happens in your home. You visualise that which you need within it, and that which you need you go and get and you create your home. The type of world you live in is created by the thoughts within your head and the type of life you live is created by the actions from your thoughts, and from these actions and thoughts you draw situations to you. You are behaving like little Gods, yes? But we need to bring love into play so that it does not just centre around one's self. The need expands from one's self to other aspects of the infinite and so you will continue to grow. This goes on into infinity.

Thank you very much for your patience. I realise it is not always any easier for you to ask the questions than it is for me to try to put it into physical words to convey an idea in response to what you have asked me. Even in giving you an idea, your interpretation of my words may be coloured, or they are coloured by your experiences. So a truer way of doing it would be to come to you through thought. That way we could convey some of the feelings as well and help you to expand your being. But we have to start wherever we are and we are all children in comparison to someone else at the end. I give you my blessings and those of my brothers and sisters of light and love, and do keep your sense of humour to the fore.

FIFTEEN

Greeting an Old Friend

Just excuse me for a moment. This is rather an emotional experience for me. I just wish to thank my old friend here. Being on the other levels and planes, it makes us rather more sensitive to experiences like this, so when we meet again it is a culmination of many lives and many lifetimes of trying to bring forward into our beings the Christ energy and to bring God into our consciousness that we may be of service to our fellow beings.

It is of course part of the learning situation to bring our emotions under control but to have great depth of feeling is part of the development or the unfoldment of your higher being and I realise I am not here simply to express my personal thanks and feelings to everyone. A great deal of arranging has been going on, I understand, from our side as well and to bring everything to a peak just for a short space of time takes some doing on everyone's part because without any of you we could not do this.

I will speak to you a little about the Christ spirit and the difference between knowledge on the intellectual level and experience from your inner beings.[1]

You asked some time about whether I have seen the man or met the man who knocked at my door. You are of course referring to Christ's spirit. Christ knocks from within you and waits for you to respond and to hear, and He continues knocking through all your lives on whatever dimension you find yourselves. This is why in the picture the door has no handle, because it is for you to find the lock and to open it yourself. You have to reach that point in your life when you are ready to begin the search consciously; because for many lifetimes you have been searching unconsciously; wandering through the illusions of the many dimensions until you come to the lifetime when at last you open that door. Then you realise with gratitude the patience, the compassion, and the love of God and all his helpers from many dimensions. I did not think it would be so difficult drawing close to the earth to hold my emotions in check and, of course, whilst we are near you working through the medium it brings back many memories appertaining to my life and my work and the help I have had from many friends in my past lives, although much of the time was wasted, time when I should have been giving forth the message which was distorted by my illusion of what was right. But the compassion of God will always give you the opportunity to put your mistakes right and when that sincerity comes from deep within, you know you have touched on the Christ spirit. Any being who becomes

---

[1] Paul Beard, the former President of The College of Psychic Studies, had been receiving the tapes for some time and had asked if he might join us one afternoon. He came down from London for the day, which proved to be a special moment spiritually for us all, and suggested that the channellings should be brought together in a book.

illumined becomes a Christed one in the way that people understand or believe that Jesus was the Son of God. Whether the Jesus who was crucified was the one that gave the teachings is open to much speculation and this is not the place for me to go into that. But any soul of a high nature who is able to impress upon the world much of God's teachings and has had to suffer for it is the sun – SUN – a sun of God, a son of the light, son – light, love and, as it was said through the Bible, so ye can become as Jesus was. All the teachings of the world have some of God's teaching in them; there is so much added to it through man's egotism, desire for power and will to lead beings in the wrong direction. But there is forgiveness in the heart of all who become illumined, because the Christ energy is there for everyone and expands way beyond the earth's dimensions. Pursue your paths, consider every move that you make, do not become self-centred, keep your humour and do be compassionate with one another; be in the joy as much as you can. Let the light grow, let it expand in this dark place. There are so many workers for light, so many willing beings. Do not knock each other down by a few unkind words, they are not necessary. Always give your love and understanding. This I know you are all taking to heart. This is why it is such a privilege for me to be able to come and be with you all here and now. We are always in the 'now'. This is something we tend to forget. That energy is always with you. You have always been a part of God. You do not have to wait for it to come to you because you are it. What is needed is a recognition, a bringing into the conscious mind of allowing the conditioning and the illusions to fall away; to see reality.

Pray to your God that you may see reality; to lead you to the light from unreality to reality. And go forward in confidence and trust on whatever level you find yourselves.

This should be what is first and foremost in your lives, but it is for you and only you to decide. This is where your personal responsibilities come in, because it is you that has to do the hard work; it is you that has chosen the path you are on, in agreement with one another, as my friend here and I have done many times. We cannot really convey to you in words, we can only share the ideas with you verbally and the only real way you can make it your own experience is through going into the silence, training your inner ear and your inner eye. Then it is *your* knowledge, it is *your* experience and no-one can take that away from you. No amount of great speaking from any other person will make any difference.

Once you have had this experience and knowledge in your fully conscious mind you will then be operating a state of being, a being of one with God, and the Christ energy is that which operates through you, in you, and which is you, through the whole of our life from birth to death and beyond.

We are part of a larger group. You are part of this group and you know when you meet someone it is like a recognition, an awareness that in some strange way the other one is part of you and the divisions fall away. That which divides has been overcome. Whilst you are still on the earth planet you may have to walk and behave as though you are still the same as you were before and maybe no-one will realise the difference. But they would be the insensitive ones, my friends; the sensitive ones will notice the difference; they will sense the light that is coming from you; they will know the love you are giving to them and they will understand when you give them compassion because they will feel it from their very depth. So whenever you feel weary and tired, and are wondering when all this weariness is going to pass, remember, remember me because I will certainly be remembering you. Now that I have done my sermonising and I've done my little bit, as they say, I do say, 'Welcome my dear friend'.

The question of the higher self: I take it it is really correct not to think of it as a being but more as an assembly or a group of beings. But does one, having cast off the outer personality, still have a shape of some sort?

You can take a shape or form if you feel the need, and if you are still on the levels and dimensions of form you can take shape in the light. If we so wish to change the shape we can, or if we wish to discard the shape or form on certain levels it would seem as though we have. We do not completely drop it altogether until we go beyond, and that is the point where I would not be able to explain any further. We see each other as light, and we see each other in the forms of density depending on what level we are actually operating on at any given time. So the closer we come to the earth the more dense we become. It is rather like putting on clothes, if you like. We draw the energy to us in whatever form we project in our mind and the higher we go we just drop them away, they're not necessary. If we do not put on a form while we are working in the lower dimensions, the ones we used to speak to will not be able to see us. Sometimes we need to operate unseen and so we can choose. Is that all right?

Is it a specialist, rather technical, business to be able to do what you are doing and perhaps not many people take the trouble to learn to do?

We are not particularly special in this. There are many who can choose to do this, but like any task that you take on you may need some training and some aptitude.

Some prefer not to come quite so close to the earth plane, some come just to observe and some come actually to work. We never come alone and we are always part of another group which is also part of another group. I believe we went into that before, did we not?

We're told that we work in the sleep state and presumably learn in the sleep state, but it's very hard to know what is the specific quality of it, the learning we do there.

The different qualities of the learning depend again on the different levels that you are living on at any given time. Part of my discussion in a previous time was that you can go to different dimensions or ..... they are very subtle dimensions; there are the dimensions and the bands of energies, and there are even more subtle bands within that, and you can be operating at any particular time in your sleep time in the more subtle bands of energy so that, for instance, you may feel that you need some instructions or experiences, particularly to do with your emotional level. Then you may, another time, feel that you need to bring more discipline into the mind or into the communication, and each level, each subtle level, is connected with the different chakras within your body. Your other bodies are all connected to these other levels, these other bands of vibrations. So that when you come out of your physical body you are still connected with all your other bodies and your inner being knows which level you need to go on at any given time. Your personality does not make the choice. It is your inner being that chooses.

If it was left to the personality it probably wouldn't bother very much because the experiences can be painful sometimes, or they can reveal the part you would rather not look at, the part you need to drop. To be able to drop your conditioning is easy to say but difficult to do, and when you do drop it, if you have lived many lifetimes with a particular conditioning deeply embedded, when you do begin to drop it, it fights. It is almost like fighting something else within yourself; you are having a battle, and when you do manage to drop it you then go through a grieving process as though someone had died. You may hear someone say to you, 'I feel as though I've been dying, I dreamed I was dying', or, 'I keep thinking I'm dying', when it is in fact the conditioning that you are dropping because it has been with you for so many aeons of time.

Is that why the knowledge of what we're doing in our sleep state is kept from us?

Part of the knowledge that is kept from you is because you have not yet developed the ability to bring it through into your conscious mind. If you experienced a great deal of the joy you would probably be reluctant to come back here. You would think to yourself, well surely if I could bring this joy through with me I would be able to go through my life dispensing love and joy left, right and centre, but then, my friend, you would not have any lessons to learn if you were able to do that; you would be already a Christed one or one whose consciousness, Christ consciousness, has risen. So to a certain extent, as you come down to this level, you become veiled again. I have to use the terminology of the earth plane. It does not fully describe what happens but I can perhaps convey to you more of an idea than anything and if it is something that really puzzles you, then I suggest you take it into your meditation and ask your guides or God. Guides are God working through other beings, and they will help you. Don't expect sudden revelations. We usually learn a tiny bit at a time.

Could you give us a picture of the group soul? One can look on it as a central consciousness plus a number of individual conscious-nesses which at times blend into one, but obviously it's only a tiny fragment of the whole thing.

The group soul – you mean as a group here and now? Yes, it is a blending of everyone's energies. I see you as energy. I see your light, and your energy is constantly moving and changing with each thought. There is a predominant colour at certain times which usually tells us of a certain type of thought that predominates. There are also the more subtle colours and light of your spiritual body which is not so clear here for me as it will be when I am not with the medium. I see things more clearly when I have left but whilst I am here I can see the subtle blendings of everyone's energies and of course you have your helpers with you. You each come with your helper or helpers. Their energies are blending and merging and lifting, and of course they have their friends and helpers and their energies, and so it goes on into an ever expanding radiating light.

So a group soul is really very large energy, not a person, however exalted?

It is focused on union with the higher being, the higher being within each soul. That is where there is a merging and a dropping away of individual consciousness and there is only the consciousness of God. That is the group soul in total union. Otherwise the group soul has many particles of itself working in different dimensions at all times, but there is the central body, being, light, love. Whatever word you apply to it does not really describe it fully. It is indescribable.

Is it possible for you to say anything – or would you prefer not to – about a life when we were on earth at the same time, which my own guide refers to in relation to me, as a sorry time?

A sorry time? I do prefer not to go into details. We prefer, in a sense, to forget the sorry times. If you have learned, and if I have learned, all that we need from those experiences, it is as well to drop them and forget, allow them to pass from your being. We have forgiven one another and we have received God's forgiveness. It does not help any further to dwell too much on the personal past, unless it is done in the sense that you can learn from it, but there is only so much that you can glean from your past experiences and there comes a time when you have to have the discipline to put it behind you and let it go.

So that's why my guide told me not to attempt to go back to the physical location involved?

Yes. You are at a stage when you need not go there, you have gone beyond that. Do not waste what precious time you have left on the earth plane by dwelling too much on that. Try to continually put your mind in the light, keep every thought faced into the light, otherwise all you will see is the shadow and a reflection; you will not see the real self.

Raynor, do you feel – we have talked about this before – is there some purpose behind all the talks you are giving and anything you would like to say about the tapes we've made and the transcripts that have been made?

The purpose is to bring knowledge and information to anyone ready to be able to assimilate what is given on whatever level they are able. We would be grateful if you could help anyone but it is entirely up to you what you do with the information given. We leave it in God's hands.

SIXTEEN

Time and Space

I will launch into a talk this afternoon which I thought would be suitable for the moment and it's to do with time and space management. Now you may think I wouldn't have thought we had to think about it but really the aspect I'm going to present to you is perhaps just another angle on something you do without thinking very much about it, but we'll try to go into it with a little bit more depth.

Now, first, you occupy your space on the planet; the space that your body takes up is that bit of space which is yours by right. By the very fact that you have a physical body you cannot help but take up a space, but believe me, my friends, if we did not have permission we would not be allowed to take up that space while we are here. Now you realise you're occupying your space within your mind, but of course we tend to forget that our aura extends far beyond the body so you are in fact taking up more space than you realise.

But because the auras do not have defined edges, many

auras can occupy a seemingly small space at one time whereas, if you had bodies the same size as your aura, you would need very large rooms indeed just to get your bodies inside. Now the body, the aura, as I have said before, is energy and of course the space that you are occupying is also full of energy, so the space is not empty, is it? In a way you could say that the word 'space' is really again another symbol for something you cannot see all the time. You have discovered that there are certain substances in your so-called space: the oxygen of course that you need for breathing and the other elements also. There are all these other vibrations which your scientists have picked up and have registered on their machines. So we realise now that space is well and truly filled; we have gone into the descriptions of different wavelengths and different bands of energies; these can pass through the space between. No, I'm not going to go in as deeply as a scientist would because I don't really think it would benefit your understanding. We are trying to understand from a spiritual point of view rather than from a scientific one.

Now, you have had to learn from childhood to manage time. We know the medium herself has a great deal of problems with time which she will not mind you laughing about. She realises that this is one of the aspects of her problems that she has to give a great deal of attention to, one way and another, but I expect most of you realise that as you increase in years and are more interested in spiritual things, the time aspect becomes more of a nuisance. Now, managing time has more to do with the physical vibrations. It has to do with your lower chakras and, of course, if you are trying to tune into your higher chakras more frequently, and to operate on the more spiritual levels, physical time becomes less pronounced in your mind. Your mind prefers to investigate on higher wavelengths. Now, if you are taking up the type of work to do with mediumship then this does become somewhat of a problem. It is in a way rather like trying to have one foot in heaven and one foot in hell! Now, I'm not saying that your homes are hell, but it does cause a division and is rather uncomfortable. It's like straddling a fence which I think all of us in the physical would consider extremely uncomfortable. But with our help, and with your willingness to learn, we can help you to deal with this, to manage that particular energy to do with the two lower chakras. When you are going into your meditation it is as well to enfold yourself in the red colour and the orange to begin with to try and keep yourself based firmly while you are operating in everyday life. Now I know most of you would prefer to go straight into the white light but again this can leave you feeling somewhat 'spaced out' when you need to operate in the physical world. It seems, too, that the more spiritual work you get into, the more appointments you have to keep, and of course the need to be aware of time management becomes more pronounced. So if you deliberately make a point of involving yourself in the red, the orange and the yellow, then go on to the green, the blue and the mauve and later the white – in sequence – this should help you in the management of physical time.

Now, when we come to make an appointment with you for the afternoon we obviously don't watch clocks. We just know, in the way that you sometimes just have a feeling that you know what the time is and you look at your watch and you find that you are correct. This is how we sense we have already made an agreement with each other for a meeting. We realise we have to try to be here for you at a certain time, so we have told ourselves, and our higher self seems to understand, this way of keeping the appointment. We have this drawing together in a group circle. We are in a large amphitheatre, with seats radiating from the centre outwards, and in the centre there is a large dome. When it is a person's time to communicate with a medium on the physical, the particular seat that they are sitting in is made up of energies which again radiate a certain colour. That is then acknowledged by everyone, or that person is then acknowledged to be the medium on our side and the one who is to contact the medium on your side, and for a time the energies are given to that particular person in the same way that you try to give your energies to the medium on your level.

When we are all ready we focus our attention on to this dome – a crystal-like dome – in the centre and we can see your circle. We see the energies and we see your shape within the energies and we can see your features. Not exactly the same way that you see each other, but we see you as light, and your form radiates the light and is in the light. And in that way we all become part of one circle, or one group, which radiates outwards as you see in Roman amphitheatres. Can you follow that? This then helps us all to live together and we can all learn the management of these energies. Again it is love in various degrees. It is love in various degrees and frequencies, and really that is your sole task while on the planet – to learn to manage these different energies for the work that you have agreed to do before you came here.

Unconditional love is the highest and purest energy. It can be seen as an intense light experienced as love and felt as warmth in the physical body. This energy should come under the direction of the higher self, which is a concentrated point of light within the radiance of Being, which is God, operating through all levels including the physical dimension. 'On earth as it is in heaven'; in other words: energy that is 'beyond', time and space individuates into particles of light within physical bodies. The infinite within the finite.

Excuse me if I am sounding a little automatic. I am experimenting with the passing over of thought to the medium in a slightly different way from usual. This is more on a telepathic wavelength. I know the other is telepathic but I am not drawing quite so close, and not using my energies to overshadow the medium in the usual way. We thought we would try it this afternoon just as an experiment, seeing that we are speaking about the management of space and time. We have not yet decided which would be the better way, but it was just another way for us to allow those on our side to see what is possible.

When you are giving out healing, you are trying to lift into higher vibrations of your own, and you're trying to tune into the higher vibrations of the soul in need, and we all agree, do we not, that it is difficult to concentrate to that degree for any length of time. But you are, I understand, all practising and trying to maintain a link with any particular soul that seems to be in need at any given time. Now bear in mind – and I know that most of you do bear this in mind, but I will say it just the same – that it always has to be God's will and it is the God within that makes the decisions.

There are times, you will understand, when you are not well, and you feel that you cannot make the correct decisions yourself, but your inner self, the deeper part of yourself, has it all in hand. But of course it is difficult, is it not, when you are physically low, to maintain the link. So this is where healers on your side, and on our side, help to sustain or form the link for that person who is going through the suffering. They have agreed to put themselves through a particular experience before they came on to this planet so that they could experience and learn whatever it is that is necessary for each individual being. And we cannot always know what it is that that other person needs to learn whilst we're in the physical body. As you develop your clairvoyance you will become able to understand a little more and realise what it is like for another person to feel the way they do, or to think the way they do. It is again a merging and a mingling of your space and your time when you come together to give healing; you are giving your time, and don't forget your time on the planet is limited to a specific amount of minutes, hours and days so that when you do give your time to someone you are actually giving them something that is of great value to you. Never underestimate that gift and try not to waste the gift. It takes a certain amount of discipline to listen and to give your time to someone who may be waffling away on something very uninteresting to you, but which may be necessary for them. It is not always what you say to someone; it is the fact that your energies are mingling with theirs and if yours are of a higher nature you can help their soul lift. We are linked with you all, at all times.

I was receiving information about the difficulty of spirits who are not experienced at passing their messages through, and that a medium's close guide is a sort of medium on that side. Is that right?

That's right, yes. That's what I was trying to explain.

Would you say that the thoughts that are being formed do not direct things like a picture? A telepathic medium – which I think most of us are – does not actually see the spirit, so a picture has got to come. Now it's very difficult to form a picture of yourself, but quite often mediums say that they see and they describe the person.

The medium on our side forms a picture for them in their mind and it's a bit like giving them a boost with energy, rather like transformers with your pieces of equipment on the earth plane. You can pass the energies through different machines to bring down the voltage so that you don't blow your piece of equipment at the lowest level, i.e. the medium. Another silly analogy, but one I think you may find helpful.

The medium who is working on our side can actually see the other person and they hold the picture in their minds and add their energies to the soul that is trying to pass the information through. Those who are not used to it haven't yet learned to manage all their energies. They may have, say, a rather strong emotional body so that if they get through they may find their emotion takes over, as mine did last week, and it takes quite an effort to hold that energy in balance with the others while you're trying to convey your mental energy levels. It's getting all the energy levels working together. Another analogy is rather like a child learning to walk: he has two legs, and he has to learn to make sure that the legs walk in balance, and it is quite difficult for the child to get them to go at the right pace. But the message has to come from the mind and through practice it begins to get the balance, the feel of the balance and the feel of what the legs will do. In a similar way it's rather like that managing your different energies through the different chakras.

If you say there's an amphitheatre for this circle, is that same method used for a medium in a church? Would they use a similar method or something slightly different?

They would use a similar method, yes. The circle is one that we find the easiest, but you can have the amphitheatre coinciding with the geometric pattern, depending on what particular wavelength or what other subject they wish to operate on. Sometimes, it is from people who are living on different planets who wish to communicate with earth. They may use a different symbol which would give them a different wavelength because they obviously are not in the same physical bodies. Some of them, again, may come to the earth in a physical body; some of them may have learned to manifest the physical body and they would again use a different geometric symbol; it is rather like a code. You will find much to do with your computers is to do with code and this is the basic principle: code.

I once saw spirit with a tall box thing and wires and different things – that's how it appeared to me – and I was told that the spirits would go in to communicate, that it was bringing the material into one area.

The symbol of the box with the wires would be energies. The wires would be the energies coming from the rectangular symbol; beams of energy.

A healer friend is very concerned that for some time, perhaps two years now, although he's been healing for many years, his guides have told him to stop. He has somebody ill in his family he would like to heal, and he wondered if there is any way in which it would be possible to communicate with his guides so that he could find out why he has to stop healing after so many years.

It is very commendable that he has spent so many years with the healing but he needs to develop in depth more of his own spiritual awareness, and he needs to conserve that energy for the time that he has left, and learn to give healing from a higher point of view, from a higher energy level. The work he has done has been necessary and very good but he needs to concentrate more on healing of the inner being, rather than the physical bodies. There is too much emphasis on healing the physical body which is very natural. Most of us would like to have a healthy physical body but from our point of view it is not as important as developing, or becoming aware of, or unfolding, unconditional love. He needs to concentrate more on being aware of unconditional love and radiating that from his being and his guides will help in whatever way is necessary. It will be better for someone outside his family to give his relative healing.

Thank you very much indeed, thank you.

Would anyone else like to ask a question? I can feel it, the mind is whirring!

When you send the message telepathically as you're doing now, it will be necessary for the medium to clothe the thought in words which perhaps will be characteristic phrases they are already used to. Is that right?

We have to use what is already in the medium's mind and their form of speaking. Possibly we do not project as much of our personality, as we operate on a different wavelength. Drawing close to the earth brings memories of our person- alities and our problems that we had to cope with whilst on earth and while we are trying to overcome that particular problem, when we come close, it does take up more energy trying to keep the personal memories to one side. As we are here to pass teachings through, and not for my personal pleasure, we have decided to try and see how we go this way, if it is all right with you. If you find that you understand, or you are quite happy with it, or if you're not happy with it please do say. I might sound a little more distant but my love is with you. Do you follow? And all the group. Do not worry, the love will come but we are trying to go on to another frequency.

I think if it conserves effort I would approve of it. Would it conserve energy as well for the medium?

We are trying to lift her away from the heavy vibrations of the earth – and it tends to leave mediums feeling spaced out – I believe that is your expression – and not able to cope with their everyday problems. So if we want new ladies and gentlemen to work for us as mediums then we must find the best ways that we can without interfering with their lives.

I can feel a question at the back of our friend's mind but it needs to be clothed in words, and maybe next time it might be as well to write it down before you come, because I do realise that when you are listening, the questioning part of the mind goes into abeyance for a little while. So it is as well to write questions down before you come.

Recently we've had UFOs in this area. Would you have any knowledge of what's happened?

Just a moment ..... they tell me that the energies play around this area frequently but it is not a subject that I am too familiar with. Yes ..... they do tell me that some of the code symbols have been relayed to your fields, and to the earth energies, and it is there for your interest and for your thoughts, and to bring the more logically minded people to the point of giving it some thought. Those who operate totally on that wavelength have very undeveloped intuitive minds. So these particular things are all connected with the ley lines and other energies that are within the earth vibrations. Energies from other planets and other levels of the infinite are being brought to play upon the planet at the moment and you will see some very interesting things in the not too distant future. But try to open your instruments, your inner instruments I mean, your being, and you will see for yourself. I'm sorry I can't be more specific than this; it is not my subject and I was just relaying information coming to me from one of my brothers who has not yet perfected the task of communicating – but he will.

Your medium and I have listened to a tape recently where a woman purported to be channelling people from the Pleiades, the stars, and the meeting got into an awful state because somebody could not accept what was said to her. I don't know if you felt or received it through the medium at all?

It is not for me to say whether one person is more sincere

than another, but there was a very good situation coming into play where anyone listening could observe that a great number of egos were battling for attention. And it was possibly a good experience for those who were prepared to open their minds and to realise that no blame is laid at anybody's door. It was an experience they had chosen. It was not inflicted upon them by anyone else from outside. The situation was set, the subject was chosen and the energies brought forward at that time were that which they had chosen to experience. There was nothing untoward. It was something for them all to learn from, even the medium.

Are you aware, or those who help you, of the future of mankind or is this something which is not yet determined?

It is not an absolute other than the spiritual. The absolute is that which you are. You have the spark, you have the light, that is the only absolute. The rest is left to the free will of mankind. This is the one planet where free will is allowed, and the different wavelengths and vibrations can come together at one point of existence. Therefore nothing can be laid down hard and fast other than that you are operating within the infinite. Again we are going into the realms of the future and as you know it is an illusion and the past is an illusion. The past has always gone, the future never comes. You are always now, you just need to realise it.

When you were talking about time and space you were referring to time being connected to the lower energies of the body. I'm one of those people who seems to have a built-in clock. I never seem to look at the clock, I don't wear a watch, but I always seem to know the time. Is it a stumbling block or something that's holding me back from progressing at a higher level?

No, my dear, it just makes you a very stable person. Just keep on progressing with your meditations and sharing your love. No, it just makes you very stable.

Time and Space

It has been said somewhere that time is to teach us that we exist, that it's one of the lessons of this earth.

Management of the energies, yes, that's right. Well, I think we have covered everything for the moment, at this particular moment in time, this little bit of space, and the management of our energies, and I don't think we feel quite so depleted. The energy does not seem to have gone down quite so quickly and it seems to be maintaining a very even balance.

SEVENTEEN

Unto Caesar

The subject I would like to discuss today is something that is probably very close to most of your hearts, if not your pocket. This is about rendering unto Caesar that which is Caesar's and the difficulty on the spiritual path in trying to bring the spirit into the way we handle our money and our possessions. There seems to be a kind of separation, as though spirit must be in one pocket and money must be in the other, but unfortunately most of the time spirit is not in the pocket and neither is the money, and as we all know this brings its problems accordingly. Now you think to yourself, 'If I devote my time to spirit surely the money should come in without me having to think about it'. Possibly that would be so if you were able to immerse your whole being in the light and in spirit but unfortunately, while we are progressing, we have one foot in heaven and one foot in hell, so to speak. This is extremely uncomfortable as most of you have probably found out. While you are thinking of spirit you find you put your money problems to one side and forget about them where they accumulate in a cupboard or a drawer.

You find, if you are thinking of your money, that you feel guilty because you're not spending time with spirit. Would I be right with a few of you? I thought I might. We had the same problem when we were on the earth plane. Now money is in fact an invention of mankind, as you all know, but the energies that circulate these pieces of paper are from man himself and also part of the God energies; they are not separate. Unfortunately we have acquired this sense of lack deep within ourselves, this lack of spirit and this lack of supplies, and it is required to let go of this deep thought, this sense of lack. There are very few of us who are actually overflowing with our material possessions. Some have a little more than others, and obviously in some other countries they are very short indeed. But in this country, to varying degrees, we all have some and usually enough to share with others. To feel that there is enough love to give to everyone, this is what we're searching for is it not? This deep awareness of the energising force of God, the love energy. Now this other energy is the same energy to a lower degree, and unfortunately the lack of awareness of God is also reflected in the way you handle your possessions because you're not only just attached to the possessions themselves, you're attached to the thought of possessing the possessions. You follow? Even if you part with an object but you still perhaps experience a sense of loss, a pain of having lost this object; it is the same with money. You may be attached to the thought of how difficult it is to acquire money to pay for the things you think you need, but most of the things you have are what you want rather than what you actually need. We can all live, can we not, on a lot less, but we still satisfy these little desires for this and for that, so we need these little bits of paper which of themselves are of no value whatsoever.

Now the pain is caused by the attachment to the thought of loss rather than to the actual loss itself, because desire is so deeply embedded within us, within our ego, our mind, our conscious mind while we're on the earth plane. You may have brought it over from a past experience, and you may have decided that in this life you will have to acquire a number of things and then let them go. You are in a way playing a game with yourself, you are experimenting as to how much power you have, and how much power does everyone else have, and how much power does God really have, and whether you can tune into this power for your own devices. But it is very similar to children in school. They are given the opportunity to learn and to understand the way things work and then they are given the opportunity to put it into practice.

But when you wish to progress along the spiritual path and unfold your spiritual being then the lessons get a little harder. You may lose everything and you may feel that the end of your life has come because you've lost all your material possessions but you haven't, you see. You still have to go on living. It is because you have identified yourself as being somebody who has possessions. You follow? If you lose that, you feel as though you've lost your life. You're probably much the same person as beforehand and you'll be much the same person afterwards except that you'll be suffering a little more. So you need to recognise what is actually happening, this attachment to the thought rather than to the actual possessions themselves.

So if you can, in meditation, cogitation and reading, if you're truly trying to become aware of what you are, drop away that which you are not, recognise that you are not this bit of money, you are not these possessions. They are separate from you. You are just using them whilst you are here. There is nothing wrong with having possessions. There is nothing wrong in having money. The problem is the attachment. Yes? So your identity gets immersed in your possessions and your money. So you have to recognise the difference, to learn to discriminate and to pay the debts you have incurred in society, but try to keep your personality out of it.

I understand. I have gone through this experience myself. There is much battling of feelings going on with this faceless body that demands things from you. Some faceless people make rules which you have to abide by or else there are consequences. You're not always sure what the consequences are but you have a feeling they are bound to be unpleasant. If you can recognise what is happening to you, it is a threat to your sense of security when someone, whom you do not know, demands something from you with which you do not entirely agree but because you are living on the planet you have to fall in with these rules to a certain extent. It is the same for everyone but you have to remember they are only material possessions and they are for helping to keep the body intact for a wee while whilst you're here. You need the food, you need the warmth, you need the housing. But do not get drawn into feeling that you are a better person or a superior person than the next because of the size of your house, or the size of your car, or the size of your bank balance. Now I do realise that those of you here today do not have quite those problems. You have learned, or you are learning to overcome them, but there are some who may hear or read these words who may not have given a great deal of thought to this. Do you understand this?

Now as to this supply and demand – a very old saying

was given to us when we were learning, that if the supply seems to be getting low give something away, but give something away that is of value to you because if you give something away that is of no value there is nothing in the gift. And even when you're paying your bills try to send each out with a good heart and with light to the person who has to spend each day dealing with all these problems. You will help those little people who have to deal day in and day out with the monetary problems that everyone has, and they are at the brunt of most people's emotions which are usually negative. You have a heart for those people who are doing their best. They are trying to help society run smoothly and you can see from your television what happens when a society is mismanaged. There are many societies experimenting in ways to support each other. These are part of the lessons that souls have chosen to experience while on the earth plane. They group together in societies and have different ways of running, or forming, the rules. Some acquire a great deal of material possessions but very little spirituality. They have made the material their God. What happens when their materials fall apart, where is their God then? If you place your God outside yourself and somebody takes it away, what do you do? You feel that you have been killed perhaps? Your life has been taken because everything material has been taken away from you. But discover that your God is deep within yourself, that even if they take your body away from you they have not taken you, the real you, because you cannot be touched. The consciousness has to be with God and the light within. Then you will be conscious of God and the light everywhere else. We know that God is everywhere, but for your purposes while on the earth plane you need to seek God within. So part of that is of discovery; is learning to realise that which you are not. You are not your attachment to *thoughts* of possessing people and things. Let these thoughts fall away and you will find each tiny thought that is recognised is like a grain of sand. It takes a great deal of grains of sand to make a beach, but this covering will fall away from you. It becomes rather like a mesh around your light. Do you follow? You have your physical body, but from our point of view these other thoughts in your aura cloud it over like a mesh so that the light is obstructed, and this causes an eddy of vibrations, of energy. It interrupts that steady flow of light and love from you and this energy which collects in little currents around you is what causes discomfort in your physical body. It begins to manifest as aches and pains or as some disease if a particular thought is held too long. Take a grasping person who is always hanging on to everything; it doesn't take a great deal of imagination to imagine what effect it would have on the physical body in time.

Now when I speak about time, this can be carried over into our next lives – and children are born with defects, are they not? Everyone feels it is most unfair, when in fact that child has carried it over from a previous life and has decided to try again. Do you follow this?

I have side-tracked a little but, as you know, when we get into this subject everything is linked with another. We only temporarily try to put these subjects into pigeon holes just for your studying, but in fact all these overlap and interlink and are all working at the same time. It's just that certain lessons, you may find, become more dominant at a particular time. You may, for instance, have several months, or weeks, or days dealing with your emotions. They may be going up and down, see-sawing; you may find difficulty in coping with other people because of your emotions, and at other times your emotions are quite calm but you're having to deal with something else.

So we try to pick up on these particular things that are happening to you and because you're in a group you may find that certain things all seem to happen at the same time to all of you. Not exactly but – you know – near enough. So we pick up on these particular lessons and we try to help you to formulate your ideas on how you are to deal with them because how you deal with them affects how you will be when you pass from this life. It affects how – maybe if – you choose to come back in another incarnation. Would there be a question you would like to ask? I have given you a great deal of thought.

Do we have a choice whether we reincarnate?

When I say choice, it is the soul that chooses and not the personality. The personality would probably not choose but it is similar to a parent deciding what a child needs rather than what a child wants. But there comes a time, on a certain level, where you will not need to come back again.

Is there any particular lesson for the Western world to learn which would be useful to it at this time? I'm talking about ideas.

Yes, you need to let go of the idea of who is superior and who is not according to material possessions. That is the overriding problem. There would be enough to go round for everyone if it was shared by those who have a great deal, but there are some men and women who have decided they want to learn about power, and unfortunately they have not developed enough spiritually to be able to handle the power. Like children, they are allowed to play with it, but of course it seems very serious to you in the physical world, does it not, if someone loses their life through somebody else mishandling power. In fact they just simply pass into our dimension. The consequences are not as desperate as it may seem on your side.

The sadness is very often for those left behind.

Yes, this lack of awareness and lack of knowledge – and the attachments – these cause the pain. And that is very real while you're experiencing it. When we say it is an illusion this does not mean we dismiss it. The illusion is very real to the one living within it, but if they could see their soul and experience the love the illusion would disappear, rather as the sun comes out and night disappears.

And how would we, on this plane, overcome the difficulties when a particular country suffers drought year after year and cannot produce its food? Will that nation have to be kept by other nations?

If the world's governments came together they should assist countries in need of food, clothing and help. There is enough to go round. It is unfortunate that repayment is always required and very little is actually made as a gift, not realising that the gift would come back a hundred-fold.

It is very difficult though when some people in those countries obstruct the help that is sent to help out. It is a very difficult matter.

I do see, I understand that, yes. They are rather like the children who will not learn their lessons and will obstruct the others from trying to get themselves organised. There is always some child like that, is there not? If you can regard them as spiritual children, even though some of them seem to behave in a most violent manner, it is because they are frightened and ignorant and need your compassion as much as those who are suffering loss in another way. That is the more difficult task, is it not, to send compassion to those who are actually being aggressive? Your natural response is to want to punish them. They will be punished, but in God's time, and they are punished by the fact that they are not aware of love, are filled with fear and anger and do not know how to get out of their situations other than by fighting.

But in the meantime hundreds, perhaps thousands of innocent people die through hunger. Is there nothing that can be done?

You talk of innocent people. It is only the soul that is innocent and each soul has chosen to go through that experience for whatever reason that they have within their being.

I have a confusion in my mind.

I do not believe it.

The soul is innocent and yet the temporary personality is only temporary and it ceases to exist at the end of each individual life. How then is there necessity for karma, unless the karma attaches to some continuing entity which cannot be the temporary personality and yet is not the soul?

You do not altogether lose the temporary personality when you pass over unless you have reached divine realisation and are God-realised in the fullest sense. You have these particles of your personality still attached to you when you go. That is why you do not become an angel the minute you pass from your body.

This I fully understand! But still the confusion persists.

But you see how the karma is still attached.

What is the karma attached to?

It is all energy. I was trying to get a picture in the mind that would be more descriptive. But it is rather like you trying to imagine one of the tiny cells in your brain and all the implications and complications of understanding how your actual physical brain works. You just know that there are certain memory cells and certain parts of your brain that do seem to function through energy passing through your cells and your nervous system. It is the energy that passes through all these things that gives life because once this energy has been removed all that is of the material falls away and goes back into another form. The energy remains in another dimension. You have to clothe yourself in a physical body to be able to live here on the physical planet. So it is the energy that is clothed with the physical. Now it is quite a complicated thing to be able to understand how the physical stays attached to the energy, but if you try to think of the magnetic forces that work through the metal and draw things to it it is something like that. I cannot give you a description that you would understand. I can only give you an analogy. It is energy that is you; it draws the material to it and it holds it together as long as you remain, or your desire to remain on the earth plane is with you, and you have allocated yourself a certain amount of time. When you – your higher self, I'm talking about, not your personality – when your higher self has decided that it is time to leave, that energy is withdrawn. Do you follow? It is a difficult subject. But all these other things, karma and everything, are energy in different frequencies. We are all energy within energy, we are points of energy within greater energy.

And when we say the higher self, is this not the soul?

That is the purest part, that is within God. You can use the word soul but others may not understand what you mean unless you explain it. They may assume that it is of a religious nature and that most people with religion seem to think of themselves as having a soul when you are in fact the soul, the light, that point, the concentrated point of light within light. You can understand possibly the difficulty of putting into words a description of a domain beyond the physical understanding.

If you think of the wind, and how many currents it has, and the same with the sea, there are many currents and eddies flowing through every tiny drop of water. You could say you are a drop of water, a microcosm containing everything within the sea. When the drop of water is thrown back into the sea it merges with the whole but it is still that drop of water.

So we're talking about the little drop of God that has manifested and come away from the central unmanifested and which has gathered on its journey many sorts of energies, and karma is one of those energies at certain levels; that there are all sorts of levels swirling round and eventually it will drop them all back again into those dimensions and become pure spirit, again to return. Would you say that's a way of saying it?

Yes, very good. Like a master computer, which is in contact with many other computers which relay the information to the main computer so that it is then available to all the other computers. That's another analogy, yes? There are many pictures and reflections of how it is; it is just for you to think of these things and clarify in your own mind the drawing away of the curtains when you feel a sudden realisation, 'Oh that is what they meant by such and such a thing'. It is a little bit at a time.

So various bodies that we are made up of are all energy as well?

Yes, yes.

So when we pass across, people say we drop one kind of energy but we still have the other energies, so the karma is attached to that?

To each body of energy, yes. It's as though the soul has been clothed in these different energies.

Is it right to think of soul as really being a part of spirit or God, which is surrounded in these energies?

Yes.

Do you eventually drop these lighter bodies as well at some point?

Yes. The higher up in the purity, when you draw away from the heavier vibrations, these other bodies drop away, these energies drop away and the karma with it dissolves and has been used up.

As we're reborn now, is it possible that we remember what we've come for and yet we don't remember it? Is it lurking around somewhere?

Yes, there is within you a memory. You could put it more truthfully and say that it is in your aura rather than in your brain. It's in the energies, in the aura, and as you tune in, as you learn to go within, you can start to become aware of the different lives that you've had. You have learned to go within and expand yourself into – your conscious mind I'm talking about – into your other bodies. You can sometimes sense them and sometimes get a sudden realisation and sometimes you can actually be aware of them in dreams.

What then of future lives?

It is a little difficult when we talk about the future, is it not, when it is only now. But what you do now can lay down what your experience will be in the so-called future. I don't think we will get into that today, that is even more complicated.

Are we interpenetrated by other worlds and with other beings of which we are not conscious?

That is true, yes. We talk of higher and lower, these are just terminologies so that we can possibly understand each other but it does not describe it fully. It is different particles of energy interpenetrating in the spaces within the other particles of energy and the finer the energy the more it can fill the spaces where the physical is. When you look within yourself and become aware of your atoms and become aware of their seeming to have a distance between them rather like the sun and the moon and the earth, and there is all this space within you, then it is a glimpse of your energy-self that you're looking at.

Would you say that you have discovered quite a few things

which are now familiar to you which you could not pass to us because of the limitations of our minds?

Yes, the difficulty in clothing my thoughts in words becomes more so the more I try to teach about that which is not of the earth. Possibly this is why I prefer to teach at first what is mostly to do with the earth plane and how to advance from that to the next dimension because it is so difficult. But when you get here you will understand it.

Do you teach on the other levels?

I do teach on the other levels, yes. It is rather like trying to explain to a child why it must go to school. It may not want to go to school; it cannot understand why it has to leave Mummy and the comfort of its own home and toys, and it makes no difference how much you try to explain to that child how it will be in another five or six years. Perhaps you will understand my difficulty. The child will understand in five or six years' time, having gone through the experiences, but in the meantime it is better for the parent and the teacher to teach the child that which is immediately in front of it, rather than wandering too far ahead into the possibilities.

Is mankind as a whole beginning to understand these things better while we are here still on earth? Do you think, on the other side, there is a feeling of lightening, or are we getting anywhere? We all seem to be fighting hard to tell everybody else about everything. Is it lightening or not?

Yes, it is. I can see a mesh of light spreading around the earth plane and of course it causes confusion. It stirs up the energies and creates a certain amount of confusion because people are presented with ideas that they are not used to and the fact that they may have to change their thought patterns and their attitudes causes this confusion in their outer lives. So it will look as though there is more increased confusion, I am afraid, but it is lifting.

It is the confusion that is making them turn to another, alternative way.

They talk about change and they always expect other people to change, but it is ourselves who have to do the changing and this is where the problem occurs. It affects their sense of security and then they become afraid which causes many arguments.

Is this what causes the violence?

Yes. When the energy comes in it tends to stir things up and make what is already there more pronounced, so if you are a very good person and already well into the spiritual you may find that you become more loving; you become more aware of love. But if you have weaknesses, say you are an aggressive person, you may find, or people may find, that the aggression is exacerbated.

EIGHTEEN

Forgiveness

I thought I would just mention forgiveness. It's an easy word to say but a very difficult thing to do and, if you think about it, one ego cannot really forgive another ego simply because the survival of the ego does not include the survival of another ego. So it is only the God within that can really express forgiveness because the ego, or the personal self, is all to do with that which is 'I, my, me, mine' and if you remain attached to a memory which has given you pain you cannot be aware of the God within. That is what keeps the pain going. It is the remembering, the memory. Say, for instance, a person has hurt you, that person then becomes a part of you and you marry. That person does not live up to expectations because the expectations were not God-realised. If their egos and their personalities predominate and again they hurt you by actions that give the impression of placing themselves first and you a poor second, they have let you down. Can you forgive them? Of course not, because your ego is interested in the survival of you; and have you really, at all times, put what they need first? Of course not! There are times when it is expedient to put their needs in front of you, but it is usually for some personal reason rather than an expression of divine love.

Now I don't say this in a derogatory manner because, of course, I have been there as well. But it is as well for you to examine this point very closely if you are aware of the need to forgive or, more to the point, because you are not forgiving. The reason that you have not been able to forgive is because you have not lifted your mind into the realms of God energy. If you feed the problem, if you constantly go round the problem, if you go over the same thought again and again, then you cannot detach yourself from it. Your problem is in not letting it go. You understand? This is where your responsibility comes in – this constant feeding of the negative. But you have to be able to recognise what you're doing before you can do anything about it and, when recognised, the next problem is how to stop it. Of course this is where meditation comes in, this training of the mind – your control – your higher self being in control of your mind rather than your mind being in control of your mind. The higher self must be the controller if you want to become God-realised, but there are many stages before you get there.

If you think of the very word *'for'* in *'before'*, it could be connected with the *'for'* in *'forgiveness'*. It is to be in contact with that original self which was before everything. To be able to forgive, you need to be in touch with that which was there originally for you to realise that these things are all part of the illusion of what belongs to you that does not come up to expectations.

We all know that we're not going to come up to expectations at some point or another, so we need to see truly, to see each other clearly, not as some God creature that has already reached God-realisation. The God is within, yes, but if those concerned were already God-realised, they would not be here. So it is having this compassion for one another in the realisation that there is a long way to go. And if you can realise this, some of the pain of disillusionment will be released, so let it go; it was all part of your learning process. You may not even realise at times that you are holding on to pain unless you look within and have the courage to acknowledge your part in whatever problem that you have in any relationship. You cannot change the other person. You have enough trouble changing yourselves. Allow them to be themselves, release them from your expectations, and you will set yourself free. If you dwell too much on what they're doing wrong you are imprisoning yourself. They're not aware of your particular problems unless you jump up and down and yell in front of them. They do not know that you are imprisoning yourself with worry about their imperfections. Let me remind you that you are on the path. *You* are the maturing ones; therefore you are accepting the responsibility and you are being given a great deal of help from all of us, from your guides and from those who walk alongside you temporarily and those who come with you all the way. We never condemn. I have been through it all myself and so I could not personally condemn anyone. I am still learning, and it is by your kind permission that I am allowed to come and speak to you about these things. So I am aware of my position in the scheme of things and it is certainly not as a superior being, I can assure you, my friends. I am fortunate in knowing and feeling and being aware of being surrounded by love, and it is love that is your life.

If you have something in your deep past that needs to be

forgiven, somebody that needs forgiving, and you say let go of it and you've learned from it, would you still continue to remember? Because if you let go, that isn't forgetting it, is it?'

No, it's releasing the memory of the pain. It is usually attached to a sense of being let down because of the expectations, and because the other person did not come up to those expectations. It is very similar to riding a bicycle; one can really only instruct so far as teaching someone to recognise the bicycle and telling them how to get on and how to start it off, but they actually have to get the balance themselves. I can use these words and at least it gets you thinking, so that you will yourself suddenly feel the balance. There will be a revelation. Something will be revealed, like drawing back a curtain; a feeling of lightness that comes from within as you let something go. It's almost as though you float upwards.

What should we call the dimension in which you now are? We have different names and it's difficult for us to know whether it's the spirit world, or the etheric world. What should we call it?

You mean from where I am now or where I'm usually from?

No, from where you normally reside, if I can use such a word!

Oh dear! I'm afraid it's rather like the different countries; each develop their language so that each may identify what they mean, and we are much the same. Well, we can give you different names but again we could be in different groups and each would provide you with different names. But to cover it like a blanket we call it the spirit world. It covers many dimensions and planes, but at this point it would not really help in providing you with names of things without the understanding of what those planes are.

In a way you understand by studying oceanography. There is so much in connection with the sea and everything appertaining to it that it is a whole subject of its own. Then there are these different planes and levels, each one a complete book in itself. It is rather similar here in that we operate on different bands. It's a bit like throwing a stone into a pool. You get the ripple and it keeps on expanding because all the energies from the other planes interlink and pass through these circles.

About forgiveness, quite often one is able to put a nasty experience into the subconscious and therefore one is not fully aware that it's there, but at the same time it is a disruptive force. How can one really clear out the mind and start afresh?

By constantly going within, steadily and regularly each day and finding something that is suitable for you to use, and learning how to still the mind so that more light can shine, possibly a prayer or a mantra will help you to raise your vibrations and to concentrate your mind. You will be led through that energy within your daily life, you will find that certain incidents will trigger off something that will help you to release that experience from your subconscious, but be ready to recognise it. Your meditation will help you to recognise what is happening. So the two things will happen at once.

You will notice when water is flowing, it flows steadily. Now if there is an obstacle to that flow, there is a lot of eddying and energies around a rock, for instance. Now the God energies flow as they do in a river, and the obstacles within, the problems and pain within, are rather like the rocks; there will be a lot of eddying of emotions. It will trigger off an emotional reaction and if, through your meditations, you have become quicker at spotting what is happening, you will be able to help with the release. Instead of being drawn in on to an emotional situation or argument, or staying within it for days, you'll be able to recognise it quicker.

Would any form of therapy help with that sort of thing?

Oh yes, there are many ways of helping, yes.

Well, I was just thinking it is possible of course to forgive. I think I've been able to do that but it's difficult to forget. The thoughts seem to stay with one, well, on and off. If they come to me I tell them to go away, being negative, but they do seem to come back now and again.

And they're still painful, are they, when these thoughts come back? So it could seem, could it not, that it's not total forgiveness yet? You say you feel you can forgive and you can't forget. It is until the memories no longer have any pain ..... do you follow that? There may be little particles still left. You understand?

It is when you can remember without the pain that you know you've truly forgiven. But this does not mean that you must be gullible in any way, you know. If you've learned from your experience you will not let people take advantage of you for their sakes in the future. It does not mean you have to be fools in any way. You have the responsibility, the added responsibility of not allowing that younger soul to repeat the same mistake with you.

Can you tell us anything about the nature of reviewing one's life when one passes out of the earthly body? We're told that we review our lives.

The good bits, or the bad bits?!

Well, when you pass over at first, you are allowed to relax and take time. You're not immediately rushed off to examine every minute particle of your life. You're allowed to rest and gain energies, much the same as you would here if you've had a shock; you would possibly be allowed to go on holiday. Well, in a way, we have a spiritual holiday so that we gain strength of mind, and when we feel ready to look back at our life and compare it with the blueprint of what we intended to do, that's what we can do. We're allowed to go into it inasmuch as we can learn or that we have the strength. And we always have someone with us; there is always someone there with loving support. We're never left totally alone, but of course while we're recapping we can feel somewhat alone because if we have hurt someone, we also experience their emotions or their feelings, because we are more aware of being part of each other, and it is a very salutary experience, my friends. And in a little way you can do the same here. If you wish to go over some parts of your life, and you really feel you have the strength to go through it and be honest with yourselves, you can actually feel as though you're reliving it, can you not?

And the horror with which one feels that, 'If only I'd known....'. But you can only deal with any situation with the awareness that you have at any given time. So that you would not expect the child in the babies' class to cope with the situations in the same way that you would in one of the higher classes. So there is always compassion. It is in a way learning to have compassion for yourself, but when you come out of it you feel again that much lighter and you feel you have gone up a notch or two.

Does one make plans at this stage as to what one might do to change or improve?

Plans in the sense of allowing yourself – let me see now – the freedom to experience the feelings and express yourself, but you allow the spirit to take you into the situations that would bring this about. You don't necessarily make hard and fast rigid decisions. They are very loosely laid out because the thought world is more fluid and when you are trying to hand your life over to the purity of God – and that is your goal, you follow? – then you allow things to unfold, you are drawn. In fact if you watch in your lives now, if you have

God-realisation as your goal in life, the situations that you will be drawn into, the people that you will be drawn to meet, will all be towards becoming God-realised. It will not always feel like it because, by the very nature of our karma, some of it is painful and some of it is wonderful, but again you have to be careful of not becoming attached, even if you're with someone whom you feel is wonderful. Walk along together but be aware that it is God-realisation that you are aiming for, not propping each other up, or continuing the illusion.

NINETEEN

Solitude and Service

Two important ingredients on the spiritual path are solitude and service. The problem is getting the right balance between the two. In most families there is probably very little solitude, so even trying to grab ten minutes out of the 24 hours each day can be something of a problem. But if you can manage to obtain just a few moments during your day that is special to you, important to you, not just something you slip in if you have the time, this is the way to develop a sense of inner solitude, so that you will perhaps develop that sense of being in your quiet space even amongst other people. But, of course, this does take time. You may be able to snatch a five minute break here and there, and go immediately into your inner space, because you have become adapted and adept at making your time with yourself of value, rather than a time which you need to fill.

So much time is just spent in keeping oneself amused, keeping the mind occupied, because if you spend too much time thinking you sense that you are lonely. I'm speaking of the people who have perhaps not progressed too far on the spiritual path; but developing the inner solitude will bring forward the awareness of the need for service. During our young lives, most of our time is spent in keeping body and soul together; there is so much time needed to be spent in providing for the body, never mind the other desires, the emotional desires, so that there is only a little time left, after amusing yourselves, for you to go within and contact that deeper inner core which is yourself. You need to contact this inner core to give yourself motivation for service rather than doing it purely for duty. You need to be able to do it for love. Service done purely as duty can be very dry and unstimulating and very wearing. If you can become in touch with the love within, all service becomes a joy, and the energy required will be there for you. Of course, there is a large gap between coming to know of the spiritual teaching and being able to do service with absolute joy. But it is part of the spiritual path you have chosen. I think you understand this and I think you have probably felt some of the joy – if not all of it. You have gone ahead with learning to contact your inner self and you have gone ahead with your service, not always quite knowing what that service should be, but with a desire to learn, and you have found when you have been doing that service that you have enjoyed yourself; you have been in joy and you have been doing service at the same time. There is, is there not, a very deep core in the British nation that work should not necessarily be enjoyable. It is something to do with the work ethic that you are only a worthwhile being if you have worked hard but not necessarily enjoyed it. This is another of the conditioning thoughts that we need to drop. Of course, as we grow older in body, and we are not able perhaps to achieve quite the same amount of service as we would like; there are the frustrations of wanting to do things but the body, as usual, interferes. You have spent most of your early days catering to the body and you have a feeling that it ought to be taking a back seat and minding its own business. In a sense, rather like a tiresome friend, the body should have got the idea by now that it should be coming under your control.

We think the darker forces are trying to interrupt our afternoon together, one way or another![1] This is again dealing with our material things like cars and heaters but they are very necessary in this cold climate, are they not? We do have memories of the problems of getting from A to B in one piece and keeping yourself warm when you get to B. Even though I spent much of my time in Australia, the part of the country that I was in did strike me as very damp at times and we did have autumn the same as you here. It's very English in character in the area in which I lived. It had many trees and we also had the falling of leaves which collected around my house in terrible amounts. They fell into the gutter and, of course, in Australia we collect our own water from the roof, so you collect the leaves along with it, which tended to flavour the water.

With eucalyptus?

Yes. The tea never tasted quite the same anywhere else, and then you also get the little life-forms in the water that wish to survive along with the rest of us but not in our bodies. We used to have filters, and you develop the attention to look in the water before you drink it just to make sure. Otherwise it was very pure and clean. That was a little aside!

The inner quietness is that which you need to allow your

---

1 There was a very noisy heater in the room!

light to expand so that when you are doing your service, the service has more effect and meaning, so that people will be lifted by your presence. You will not realise, perhaps, that it is your presence that counts, but they will have a feeling that meeting you has had a deeper meaning; they will feel uplifted. They will not necessarily know why, but it is a very necessary part of your work, this unity, this sense of unity. So that when you meet people you have not met before, as our friends here do, there is a sense of unity and harmony which is not easily achieved in a group of strangers. To be able to sit with several other human beings and immediately feel in harmony and at one indicates that they are at a point in their lives where they can be sensitive to the special vibrations of yourselves.

Do you have anything to say to the medium that may be of assistance to her when doing that sort of work?

Just trust that we will be with her when necessary. We will help to bring forward confidence and the ability to control her nerves, but just practising coming along with yourself and listening would be of great benefit for her. She can come in with you and sit quietly and take note of how it feels and she will become aware of impressions within the mind of what could be said, and if you will allow her now and again just to say a word or two, I'm sure it will be of great benefit to both of you. I do not mean that she should take over in any way; this is not our desire. We will be there to lift the vibrations within the place that is visited but we will not necessarily need to speak. You understand? We will try to impress upon the medium as your guide does for you. In this way, it would be a form of training. It is good for all mediums to work with other mediums so that they can learn. There is always humility, a need for humility so that one can learn.

A Hindu gentleman suggested that a person can reincarnate as an animal.

When you say that they reincarnate as an animal, it is not the human consciousness that is reincarnated in the animal. There is an element of truth in this thought but there is a misunderstanding of the actual way. It is as though part of the being still continues to operate on our side but there is a tiny element that may need to come back and take the form of a lesser being, but not in a way that one would take form in another human. So you could say yes, and you could say no, or you could say neither. This is part of the problem and part of the understanding, or lack of understanding, of what or who actually reincarnates because the whole of ourselves does not reincarnate. That is, I'm afraid, as much as I know. I will enquire. It has been something that I personally have wrestled with for some time, both in the physical world and on our side, and even on our side there are differences of understanding – on our level and on the lower levels. I think it is something we will not fully understand until we raise ourselves into another band of energies.

So if you have the total sum, the higher self, the whole soul, parts of which, as you say, reincarnate, but not all of it at the same time, then possibly, if a soul has not advanced too far, there may be certain parts of it that are still left from back at the time of reincarnating as an animal? It is said that we go through the animal stage prior to the human stage, so that there could still be parts of your total self that might still appear as an animal. Now does that seem to make sense?

Yes. The soul may have made one very serious mistake in an otherwise spiritual life and that part of himself that caused the mistake in the first place will still need to be purified.

Are you saying that the higher self, the whole bit that we come from, the whole part, could be a mixture of human and animal?

Yes. The human is still very much on the level of the animal. They are not that far in advancement of the animal.

Unfortunately, mankind on the whole does tend to think of itself as rather superior and unfortunately the Bible has perpetuated the idea that animals are only there for human use rather than sharing the planet as a whole.

Is that why, in India, they consider the cow and other animals as so sacred that they will not kill them?

Yes. It is that element of God within the animals that the Indians hold as sacred, the cow being symbolic of the mother. In India, the female is as important as the male in that their God does not exclude the female in the same way that some religions here do.

But in India they are killing little girls.

In the same way that not all Christians have reached perfection not all Indians have reached perfection. There are many who will struggle against their spiritual teachings because of poverty and the need to keep their bodies together, which is a great motivator in starvation.

If a part of the soul, say, was a vivisectionist and did rather awful things that were really not helping anybody, maybe another part of his soul might have an incarnation where he might learn by becoming the animal that had had that happen to it.

The man who may be motivated to help people yet causes a great deal of suffering to animals possibly needs to extend his awareness into that field.

We need to look at this greater self more. We think of ourselves as complete and we're not.

Even on our side we are aware that we're not. I have always found there are many realms beyond our level that make us more aware of how little we know. The more I have learnt the more I feel how little I know. Even though you feel at times you are on the brink of knowing everything, that all knowledge is just there, just beyond, each time you reach the knowledge there is always just a little bit further to go. There's always another mountain to climb.

Talking to groups, I'm very much aware that I'm only talking at the level that I have reached and that therefore I may say things which I later find to be untrue, and I wonder about the responsibility for this. Is it wise always to say, 'Well, this is just an opinion; it is your responsibility to decide'?

Yes. That is why I stress very much personal responsibility. All you can really say to people is, 'This is what I have come to understand, this is the amount of information I have received and this is after a lifetime of seeking,' then proceed to say that you are aware that there is a great deal more but to advise each person to take personal responsibility for what they do with the information they have and always to keep part of their mind open and ready to drop whatever has to be discarded. Anyway, you need your crutches when you're crippled and it would be foolish to try and walk without the crutches, would it not? Yet, when you are healed you would be foolish if you did not drop them. Likewise there is certain information that is needed to prop us up until the time comes when we no longer need it. In the same way people who go to church need their church and it would be cruel to disillusion them without having something else to offer. If they were not ready to accept that which was offered they would be as crippled as people would be without crutches.

If people could only become aware that their knowledge is only partial! The problem comes when any religion or sect claims that they have all the knowledge and then they force you to follow them, and I do mean force – you know, accept it or be excommunicated; that is force.

I recall that you have past feelings of being forced in your Spanish life.

Yes, that is one life in which I wrought the devastation of forcing and being forced.

I'm interested, as everybody is, to know whether changes are impending on the planet Earth in the way of spiritual development. I wonder if you could see signs of this spreading on planet Earth?

I believe it is a continuous process and that it has never really stopped; it just seemed to stop! There is obviously some development and there is a resistance to the old and resistance to the new, so it would seem that there is more conflict because of both these situations. But there are pockets. We seem to see that there are more definite pockets of people working in the light, but there is also a stirring up in the pockets of darkness and it is rather like a dividing of the sheep and the goats. I can see the drawing away of the different groupings and then it is more obvious for each side to look at the other and say, 'You are not one of us', and then they fight. It is very mixed up and there are areas where it is all very mixed up and other areas where they are drawing apart.

I believe you said recently that we shall be challenged in our views and that we must centre ourselves. Do you have any particular knowledge of how we shall be challenged?

No. I'm not allowed to say. No. Whenever the light pushes forward to make itself known then obviously it attracts the dark. If you are not being very effective in the world then the dwellers of the threshold don't bother you too much, but the minute you become an effective worker for the light then you attract these dwellers on the threshold who will motivate other beings, who are not controlling their thought-forms, into attacking you verbally, fortunately, not in any other way. This is where you need a lot of courage and this is why I stress the need for a firm foundation, a firm basis, from which to move so that you are sure within yourself of what you say.

Is there any particular reason why drugs are so much in the forefront of our society?

Yes. The young ones are seeking the life that they were given, and life in society, even for those who are seemingly successful, is not enough. It does not satisfy that need within and the desire to use drugs is a kind of short-cut. They can become aware of their inner selves but they can also damage their other bodies, their astral body. They can leave holes so that when they do come into our side their astral body and mental bodies are damaged and they need healing; a great deal of healing.

When they try to get these thrills, are they seeking something which they could get in spiritual terms?

They may not know that that is what they are seeking when seeking to feel less ignored, less inferior, less separation. Youngsters collect in groups, do they not? It is only perhaps when the addiction becomes serious that they cannot look after themselves properly and are alone, but the majority are just experimenting. They are usually within groups of like-minded beings and they enjoy the sense of unity, the sense of separation being temporarily removed. That pain of being alone is diffused, the edges are not so noticeable.

It's being alone that teaches us. You've got to learn to be alone to be able to move into a group.

Of course, the youngsters are often not given any grounding. They're not even aware of their divinity or even of the possibility.

We worry it will lower the moral fibre of the whole of civilisation. That's the trouble.

Yes, yes. It's this 'instant' everything; give me now! We

just have to keep pitying them. They are not totally lost, you understand? It is only pain which makes it seem like an eternity and that their lives will be very short. But, of course, we forget there is infinite love.

Which goes on eternally.

We've recently seen on television a man who is counted as a mystic and it made me realise that many years ago, when I was very young, somebody said that I was a mystic, which I denied. But of course, I've realised over the years that that's exactly what I am. I wonder whether I should write down exactly how I got there and what my feelings are; whether it would be of use as coming from an everyday type of person?

I think that would be very good. People are usually interested in learning how somebody got to their present position. Because you are passing on the spiritual teaching, there are many who would recognise in your experiences situations they go through.

I was only going to pick out the things that referred more to the spiritual path during life.

People would be interested to hear the difficult parts because those are the parts they will recognise in themselves. The fact that you have become aware, in spite of your difficulties, will help them in coping.

Do you still keep up your old interests in science and how the scientists are progressing or have you decided to drop that?

No, I've decided to drop that for the moment, because it is so different from this point of view. I am now more interested in spiritual aspects. I still do some painting now and again; a mixture of colours in the mind. You can use brush and paint, so-called paint, but it is more a mixing of the energies, if you understand.

TWENTY

Thought-Forms

Thought-forms. It is interesting, even upon suggesting the term thought-forms, to observe the energies around each of you. The types of thoughts you tend to think for any length of time build up a certain form of energy and they are in a state of continual change, of flux, of intensity. The intensity of the thought as it is sent out will depend on how much of the emotional is behind each thought. If you are sending it at someone it can shoot out in the form of a direct beam of light or it can be a bit on the negative. It will be in various shapes, you see?

Anyway, the thoughts that we give out do tend to resemble the way fish swim through the water. Some of the thoughts just meander around. There is no great power behind them so they just meander around until they evaporate, or are withdrawn, or change form. Now this is leading up to understanding a little more about the importance of keeping a check on your thoughts and possibly, as you use your mind for healing purposes, in sending out light to those in need. Any thought of a positive nature is used, and is useful in lifting up the surrounding energies. It helps to lift and clear away the darkness. It helps to lift those who are in need and are unable to lift themselves. The light-forms collect around the person in need and eventually interpenetrate their aura.

Now you can see, can you not, the dangers of negative thoughts because if you continually put a person in your negative thoughts you are, in a way, holding them back. So you would need to observe yourselves as you talk to each other, and be aware of what kind of thoughts you are entertaining at any given moment. It is so easy, is it not, for us all to slip into a nice little chit-chat about one another, and this is very much a human condition and none of us are any exception to the rule, I'm afraid. But we are all becoming aware, are we not, of these dangers, so try, if you do have a negative thought of anyone, to follow it up by putting them in the light, or trying to understand why they are the way that they are, and how they came to be that way. What was it in their life, or in their past lives, that led them to be the way they are? In this small way you can help yourselves. You are dropping the negative thoughts, you are helping to keep the dwellers of the threshold at bay, you are making their task considerably harder which is all to the good. Even they have their place in the scheme of things; they test you in a way because if you make the statement that you are on a spiritual path and wish to improve you may well be tested, my friends; we usually are. Now to go into the business of thought-forms on higher levels, we are of course building the centres of light on the different levels so that you can all link up into this light to use it whenever you need for your healing, you see?

Can you see them?

No. I can just sense them ..... very gently.

Water is used while we are doing the work here. It helps with the energies and the thought-forms. We collected the energies around the mediums and we, in a way, anchor ourselves to you by thought and we draw energy to the particular medium who is working, and water in some way helps. It is a little technical and I will not go into it just at the moment.

In conditioning your mind through meditation, you are trying to lift yourself into a finer vibration above the tiny thoughts which are rather like children in a playground. They settle down. They, in a way, become aware of the finer energies which have an effect on these tiny little thoughts which are pushed to one side. The wavelengths of the brain change form and you become aware of your other bodies and your other selves. This feels like an expansion so that you are extending yourselves beyond your physical and you become aware that you are more than just your physical being; you are expanding yourself into the infinite, and by tuning into those higher vibrations you link yourselves with the higher beings from the other dimensions. They will be drawn to you and, if you are serious in your desire to do the work, they will come to you and help. They will not so much come to speak through the medium as be with you and help you to generate more light and more love. When they see that your desire is sincere and that you are putting it into practice – just at that moment when you feel you are succeeding – comes one of the tests and you are thrown in at the deep end and faced with something usually of a darker nature. I am just warning you of this, my friends, so that you will not be taken by surprise when this happens. Do not immediately assume that you are the worst person possible. This is just something surfacing from your past and you may not remember the details; just deal with the emotion that surfaces and beware of the type of thought-forms you become aware of. Surround yourself with light and you find that the darker energies will disperse fairly quickly and the more you put this into practice the quicker you will overcome the problem that you are facing.

When you have to go out into your daily work you will be bombarded by other thought-forms. Many a time you will find that this will have a very wearing effect upon you. You are becoming more sensitised; you will become more sensitive to other people's thoughts and other people's emotions. These may feel like your own for a little while until you identify where the thought-form is coming from. This is why it is necessary to dip into your meditation regularly. This builds up and strengthens your nervous system so that the higher energies, as they come through to you, will not over-stimulate you, because they can be very stimulating and they will bring up to the surface your weak points. I'm touching a little on that which we have spoken of before but I don't think it is ever wasted. This I have found in the past.

You've mentioned the words 'the dweller on the threshold'. I don't fully understand.

These are beings who are still caught up in negative vibrations and cannot see the reason for moving away and they tend to hover around the earth planet. They are rather locked in on the thought-forms, if you like, and they try to draw satisfaction in a rather nebulous fashion from people who are still in the physical body. They draw close and can become lodged in your auras if you are not aware. In fact some of the people who find their way into mental hospitals have in fact probably acquired one or two of these beings. It is simply that they are lost and do not wish to hear any suggestions from other people on the other side as to how they can draw away; they do not wish to draw away and they are allowed to choose. Maybe they will learn – we hope they will learn – and some do and are drawn away when they have had enough.[1]

Would it be helpful for psychiatry if this knowledge was available? I've had to sit on cases where someone had heard voices in his head telling him to smash a window or hurt somebody. Is this possibly the result of obsession?[2]

Of course not every time. It would help if the psychiatrist was able to see or even if it was accepted that clairvoyance could help in this way. But some of the psychiatrists are aware but they dare not speak of it, at least not while they're working.

Do you have any work to do at any time with people in the dark regions?

We do not go alone, we go in groups, so that we have the energies to support one another.

How could we help someone, whom we may feel has another lodged in their aura, to remove that other person?

Well, of course, if you talk to the person that is one way, but if they will not listen then all you can do is to put them in the healing light, or maybe one of your clairvoyant people may be able to contact that being and speak to them. Or you can ask one of your guides, if you are in contact with them, to see if they can help.

Sometimes it is very difficult and they are very obstinate, particularly if they've been there for quite some time. It's

---

[1] Raynor Johnson's use of the term 'dwellers of the threshold' is not the same as the Theosophists' 'Guardian of the Threshold': a powerful figure whom it is necessary to encounter before entry onto an advanced spiritual path.

[2] This member of the circle is a Magistrate.

almost as though they've grown tentacles which lodge very deeply. They look as though they have hooks and this energy comes out with hooks on; it locks in in some form and as fast as you undo one hook another tentacle comes out and hooks on again so that you need someone very knowledgeable on our side who knows how to help without becoming entangled themselves because there is the danger that they may attach themselves to you instead. So don't think about them more than necessary. If you are aware don't allow them to stay in your mind. Be very aware that you're strong enough to deal with this, otherwise hand it over. Possibly those who are very seriously affected need to be with a psychiatrist. Do not try to deal with that on this level yourselves.

It's going back to seeing expertise where it's available?

Yes, that's right.

Do electric shocks, given to cure mental trouble, sometimes incidentally remove things from the aura?

Yes. It has its for and against. It does quite often remove the offending person but it can damage the aura of the patient.

This has done irreparable damage.

They can be helped by a great deal of healing for quite a long time otherwise it may not be fully reparable.

To leave them open to further occupation.

That's right, yes.

Would that also perhaps follow in the case of some who have heart surgery? Leaving holes in their aura – they sometimes change personality following the surgery.

You're correct.

Do you read books any more?

Yes, but it's much easier. You have the books but somehow you absorb and feel the information that you have within the book. We absorb it in a somewhat different way from when we are on the earth plane. You can actually feel and see the intention of the author and in a way you almost become one with the author when you are reading. I say reading, but it is not exactly the same as we would do it on the earth plane.

We get a whole new dimension to taking in information, don't we?

Oh indeed. Yes, I've many times thought it would be wonderful when on the earth plane just to hold the book and be able to absorb it overnight. It would save a great deal of time.

Are you in contact at all with the group known as the White Brotherhood?

Yes. This is extending around the planet now. We may be called different things in different places but it is basically that.

Incarnate versions of the Brotherhood?

Both.

I think sometimes they call themselves the Silent Brothers.

Yes, we are encouraged to work quietly behind the scenes. It helps us to control the sense of self-importance which is very easily developed and we are not above becoming attached to that form of vanity, or the glamour of it, as they say!

You say you draw the energies to the medium working. I know it may be a very technical answer to this question, but could you possibly summarise it to give me some understanding of how you do this? Also you said, 'Imagine a centre of light on which you can draw in your healing'. How do you do that?

I think we have come back to the problem of how to ride a bicycle. You identify the bicycle, you instruct the pupil on how to go through the motions: if you do this and that it will go forward and you will find that you will balance. In the same way we teach you about meditation; you sit still in the silence, and you learn to control your thoughts, so that they come under the direction of your soul. Your soul is light and is love, that is the central point within you which is God, and the spark of God within you is in contact with the infinite God or universal infinite.

But again the balancing has to be done by yourself and is not something that can actually be taught. I can tell you all the things which you can try to do. We can draw close to help you by our very being, our vibration and the state that we are in, of a higher nature, so that by being drawn into your aura we can help you to experience a little bit of that which is beyond and this will be retained in your memory and help you with your motivation. Do you follow this?

Do you foresee, during our travels, being able to do some work on the way?

Your work is to love and to just be, and to work on yourselves and to generate more light wherever you are by tuning to your higher self which will guide you into situations where you can either be of help or can learn.

You will obviously not be able to communicate as easily as you would here but there will be many people that you could introduce to your particular thoughts, of course if it is a Catholic country you may have to be a little careful. Be sensitive to when and where.

I don't find it very easy to lift off during meditation. Have you any ideas?

Persistence. Most people have the same problems. A lot of the time is examining yourself but the greater God will come and help us.

One is able to gain a lot of knowledge in the course of one's life and the most difficult thing to do is to sort it and retain it. How can one improve one's ability?

Yes, there is this problem as the physical body becomes

older and less supple and the cells deteriorate. All you can really do is just go quietly within and keep the mind active when it is necessary, and your mind will sift through all the information that you have and will retain that which is necessary, and drop that which is not. But other than the normal things you have to attend to, make sure that the nutrition is right and that you are not where there is a great deal of pollution; stay close to water if you can, where there is more fresh air. Apart from the usual things and meditation I'm afraid it depends on your karma.

You could visualise the colours. You could fill your being with golden light. Do not allow negative thoughts to stay with you, examine them, see where you are at fault and then say that they must leave; you do not need them.

TWENTY ONE

Nature of Evil

Now I want you to be very strong in holding the light within you today because we really should have a look at the nature of evil. It is better to know the Devil – I say 'the Devil' but in inverted commas; it is just an expression that is used and is not really a man with horns or a tail. It is the absence of light, the absence of love and the absence of knowledge. You may think that whatever is going to damage your body, your mind, or your emotion is evil, but if you think about it, the sea, the fire, anything material, can be a danger to your body. You may even consider it as evil but it does not have a mind of its own, it just simply is. Water is simply water and fire is simply fire. There are elementals but this is not the same as being. Fire does what fire is supposed to do, and water does what water is supposed to do, but of course if they both destroyed your body you may be forgiven for believing that they were evil.

I am going to mention this incident that you have been

talking about[1]. You may or may not wish to use it in the book but you may be able to work around it. This is a very good example of how justice will be done and how really we, as humans, do not really need to apply justice in the punishment sense as we do on earth because the punishment comes round, does it not?

This is a very good example of how these youngsters have followed each other down through time perpetuating their karma, and how, if you make a curse instead of forgiving someone for hurting you, you can end up doing that which you have cursed somebody about. You will find somebody you have cursed somewhere along the path of time and you may fulfil that curse without the memory of why you actually cursed that other being. So if you do not try to work through the pain and the misunderstanding that you have when somebody hurts you, or one of your family, then this case shows how it will go on and on until one of you can become aware and cut the link.

It is something that has stirred your nation from one end to the other with varying intensities of reactions from both sides, both the parents of the child that was killed and the parents of the two offending children, and people are taking sides even within their different families. Some will follow the text of an eye for an eye and a tooth for a tooth, and others will follow the teachings of trying to forgive. Of course just saying that you have forgiven doesn't exactly mean that you have forgiven, but each person who has passed judgement on the situation will be laying up more karma for themselves. It is a way in which they will learn eventually, not necessarily in this lifetime, of the dangers of passing judgement without knowing what has gone before.

---

[1] The murder of the Bulger child

Nature of Evil

Of course it all seems extremely uncaring, and there's a hint of the word 'evil', as though that were a separate entity. But the thought-forms – we're back to thought-forms again – the thought-forms that people are projecting into the surrounding etheric world – and some of these thought-forms are filled with a great deal of anger and hate – collect together; they are drawn together as like to like and they form pockets of energy where there is no light; they block out the light. In those areas where people collect with very dark thoughts and feelings, the energy collects around that place and penetrates and permeates every other physical object within the vicinity. So it would seem that even the buildings and the very bricks seem to have a life of their own. As you know, you can go into buildings and access the energies if you are sensitive, for which you are all developing the ability. So you can see the responsibility we have for the kind of thoughts we think wherever we are. This is why I say to you at times to take the light with you, because the more you surround yourself in light the more you can affect the surrounding area that you're in, and you can leave your energies and your imprints upon all the physical objects around you and you can affect the people you're with. But you need to grow stable so that you will be able to hold the light even if you're challenged, by being in a room full of darkened people, so that your light affects them but their darkness does not affect you.

So again you realise the great responsibility you have by coming into this knowledge. It is an added responsibility because you cannot say from now on that you did not know. I'm afraid even by saying that you forgot is no excuse. It is understandable because we are all still at the human level, and this is why we must apply this understanding to other souls who have not yet reached the point on the path that we have. In a way this shows why people should make more effort to understand that the beings whom they believe to be inferior to them are only at the point they once were.

You recognise that something is not right and one has to have the courage to say so. This does not necessarily mean that you are going to be drawn into a fight about it but you must state quite clearly the right from the wrong. I know we discussed things as being relative but we are, are we not, aiming for the highest point, the highest ideal within your mind and the higher understanding of your God within, or your infinite universe, or your infinite unconditional love, whatever name you wish to apply to the eternal. There is a point that is pure goodness. Anything below that is relative.

I was a magistrate for many years. We understand that people are all at different levels but it was always thought that the purpose of judicial proceedings was (a) containment; (b) rehabilitation and (c) deterrence.

It is not helpful unless you can actually get the person to understand; this is the true deterrent. If they cannot understand why they must not commit a certain act then you have to contain them to protect other people or the other being, but one of course needs to try to teach them why they are contained, otherwise they just end up with a sense of self-righteous indignation, a sense of injustice.

But of course some do not have the mental capacity to understand and they, when set free, commit the same act again and will again have to undertake more reactions to what they have done and all that goes with it.

What I was thinking and perhaps didn't make quite clear is that containment and rehabilitation is fine for the people who are caught, but the object of deterrence is to deter people who are not committing crimes from starting to do so. How much importance should society put on this?

I think a lot of the deterrents are really for people who are going to do something that is wrong anyway; they will very rarely be put off by a deterrent because they have it within their beings to commit the negative act in the first place. If you are an angry man you will find a situation whereby you can justify your anger. Most people think that the situations come and then you become angry but it is because of the anger within already that the situation is drawn to you so that you can express your anger, and if you do not think clearly you will give yourself a self-righteous reason for being angry. It is very subtle and needs a great deal of thinking and going deeper than thinking, so that you could feel the essence that has been clothed with words. It will not be grasped in a moment, not deeply.

We're acting like partially sighted people who don't know, half the time, what's going out.

Yes, that is true, yes, but we can only do what we can with the information that we have at any given time. So each society struggles along and hopefully learns from its mistakes, and knowledge, then, unfolds.

When this incident of the child murder originally happened I tried to see if I could put some love in to help in the area. Just offer it. It was as if boards were being thrown up that wouldn't let me through and I knew that they represented karma. All I asked to do was to leave the love at the doorstep and it would be used. How would that have been used in that instance?

The love?

How would it have been used in spirit?

It is used in a similar way that you would use dressings on a wound. It is applied a bit at a time, a fresh dressing as the healing goes on. If you have a physical wound, for instance, you need to change the dressing regularly and the healing goes on slowly, does it not? In a way we can apply the love energy in a similar way. If we channel too much of the energies, high energies, before the being's system is ready to contain it, it can over stimulate the being and stir them up so that their weaknesses come to the surface, but if all those weaknesses come to the surface too soon and all at once, it can cause more damage than if applied at the intensity with which the being can cope. Do you understand this?

If I'm feeling that something should be left on the doorstep for the two who are now going to go through many years of imprisonment, and if we're not going to stir it up too quickly, do we use the same method?

It is as though you're pocketing, or depositing pockets of energy there ready for their helpers – because they have helpers as well – to help them as they grow in understanding of what has happened to them. They will not remember very much of their past lives, obviously, and they will probably not understand fully for some time what the fuss is about. They will be aware that they have done something for which they are being punished and which everyone else is telling them is very bad. A little light will have to grow within them a little bit at a time as they grow each day.

Is it worth while to do that?

Oh yes. You can help by this energy or love that you send which can also help to soften the attitude of the people who are working with them, so that they will decide to help them rather than to apply revenge.

And of course the other boys around them as well.

Yes, and any other youngsters that they will have to live with, who will have heard the other adults speaking and will believe that it is right to torment these two boys without looking at their own failings. They will project all their own failings on to these boys so these boys will have to carry all that as well.

Of course there are so many others – who cannot be in the

papers as were these two – who need that sort of help as well.

Yes, so it is just focused on these two particular boys.

So we should send out to others as well?

Yes, yes.

There is a possibility that these two boys, when they grow up into manhood within Detention Centres, will receive rough justice from men inside who just loathe the thought of children being attacked. Is there any way that these two can be protected in later life, when they meet this condition?

Only through their own thought-forms and their karma. These other men are all projecting their own negativity on to other people. This is what we as humans tend to do to one another. It is much easier to look at someone else's failings and concentrate on them rather than look at one's own, because someone else's failings always look much worse; because you know a little bit more about why you did something, but we very rarely know the whole reason why another person does something. Do you understand? You see, we do not always know why we have done something ourselves; we may be taken over by an impulse and of course there are these dwellers of the threshold who will push, and these two boys probably had some shadow figures around them.

I have not myself seen but I would imagine, from what I was told, they had some shadow figures urging them on and the boys followed impulses without fully realising. You know how things escalate and once you get two or three in a group, they follow. It's as though their energies collect together and with the others being around them, they seem to follow the impulses more; they follow their sudden thoughts. Their backgrounds were not very stable, they are not stable and the families were not stable, therefore they follow. Their minds are like butterflies.

That situation can be seen more readily in a pack of dogs.

Yes, yes, you would. We as humans are not that far above the animals in following our impulses. It is only by coming into tune with your higher self that you begin to draw away from the animal aspect of your human self. You are in fact growing up.

One understands there is perfect justice in the universe so I would have thought that these people on the threshold would have gone through a procedure in the next world where they were not allowed to cause further trouble in the earth world, but would dwell in a dark place where they were trapped, and from which they needed to be rescued. Are these the people then who perhaps have put off going to that stage and who hover around the earth and do these things?

It is as though some of them are on the borderlines, on the border surroundings, in the vibrations and energies, and they break through in certain areas and are drawn to areas where this single vibration is being given off by humans in the body. We are not a long way away from you in one sense and you are simply on a lower vibration whilst in the physical body. Your soul energies still exist in our dimension on whatever level, and it seems to be as though our consciousness can travel, so to speak, up and down the scales. It is very difficult to describe these different dimensions and how we move around but if you, when you're in meditation and you are trying to become one-pointed in your consciousness – when your mind has not wandered off, and there's a kind of vacant space, when your thoughts are not drifting like different waves – there comes a point where you feel as though you are at one point of consciousness within the eternal consciousness and it is as though you are aware of that which is above, behind, in front, everywhere; as though there is nowhere where you are not, and if you want to transfer your point of consciousness to another part of space one seems to be able to do this through thought. So you are clothing – as you come down through the vibrations – you are clothing that point of consciousness with a heavier vibration, so that you can be seen by other beings on that particular level, so that when you come to the earth plane you have clothed yourself in the physical. This again is how babies are formed, so that we can interact with one another whilst on the physical plane or whatever plane on which we happen to be fulfilling our karma.

Will these 'dwellers on the threshold' who can do this, ever need to reform? Can they carry on doing this indefinitely?

We do not leave them so that they are never given the chance. In the same way that you do absent healing for some, we can do that also, and different groups of us can come into their domain and we can begin to try to work on them individually. If they are beginning to cause more havoc, we try to surround them like a coral, but in light, so that instead of the darkness nibbling away at the edges of the light, the light nibbled away at the edges of the dark. You follow?

Yes.

And it is because they do still have the spark of God, that there comes a point when even they become sickened by this perpetual darkness and all that goes with it. I won't go into details of that, we do not wish to bring the vibrations any lower. We are maintaining an even keel, are we not? We do not wish to draw ourselves down, any of us here, but we need to understand as much as we can.

I was trying to send some love to these boys and I seem to have to send a very, very deep purple.

That is a cleansing colour, yes, we use a purple for cleansing places when we are working.

It was a very deep purple.

They need something stronger and nearer to them.

TWENTY TWO

The Purpose Which the Masters Know and Serve

The purpose which the Masters know and serve. These are profound words and are the purpose of the Masters. That is the reason why we are here. We are all trying to serve the purpose. I know I jokingly made comments some time ago about purpose, but the purpose comes from deep within, the awareness and realisation of your divinity, and it is in this purpose that we all serve the Divine, to help other beings become aware of their divinity. This purpose should be the one sole aim in life, but of course if you have no awareness of divinity, or even that there is a Divine, then your life can go round in circles without any real sense of purpose. You take many paths until you become aware of the path. You can take many side roads which will eventually lead back to the main path but this may take you many lifetimes, many lifetimes. You're allowed to pursue that in which you are interested but in doing so you may lose the real reason for being here. In the situations you find yourself – and some of them can be very earth-shattering, I think the expression is – it is almost as though the soul is trying to shake the ego free so that it will drop away; so that this whole can come through, so that you can begin to question yourselves.

Do not just take the way that you have been thinking for granted; do not assume that because you have done something for years and years you must continue this way. Those moments of illness, or grief, or loss of any sort, are the soul's opportunities. It is then that it can most likely be heard. It is unfortunate that as human beings we do not respond to the Divine too well when we're happy. We tend to put it on the back burner. We think we will worry about that later, not realising that later comes sooner than we think; that the time we have in the human body is not really very long and the opportunities are past before we really know that they were opportunities. We mostly tend to see them as interruptions in our enjoyment of life, do we not? Things that we would perhaps put off rather than experience. But it is – and you know this yourselves – a great opportunity to think more deeply about what you do, and what you think, and what you say, and for learning to trust that little bit of divinity within yourselves, and to realise that the guidance is there to help you with your purpose so that you also may serve the masters in the full knowledge and awareness of your divinity.

Your whole life would be a seeking to merge your divinity with the whole. But in a way it is whilst you are here that your little spark of God learns to grow up, in a sense. You ask if the soul is perfect and I would say yes, in the same way that an embryo can be perfect, but the embryo needs to grow to be a man or a woman, to be perfect as an adult. In a way, this does not fully describe it, but it may help you to understand what we mean by the spark of God and why, if it is perfect, does it need to come here! Perfection can expand, it is perfect while it is small and it is perfect when it expands, but on this level you would not truly fully understand until you have reached realisation. But I realise that as humans we seek to try to understand something of the Divine because we have been told that this is what we should do.

Try on the personal level, try to do more of your meditations if you can. I realise that in your busy schedules it is not always possible but if you could extend your meditation times this will help you to make a stronger link with your God within. Do make sure you regulate your rest times. Do not allow other people to manipulate you into a kind of life where you must feel as though you're rushing here and there.

I must also speak to the medium about this. There is a need to regulate more, so that your bodies do not wear out before you want them to. The energies that will play upon your nervous system can make you feel somewhat overstretched at times, so this is why you need to take brief rests in between periods of moving around. Twenty-four hours a day I know does not seem long enough to get everything in, including sleep, but it is most important and I have been asked to stress this: learn to trust your inner awareness a little more each time. You will receive much criticism in the future, I'm afraid. You will be challenged on what you have said or helped to perpetuate, but this should help – your meditations and your rest – to ground you, and give you a solid base from which to work. You must not allow anyone to knock you off your solid foundation. Accept what people have to say. They have the freedom to choose and they have the freedom to express. Discuss by all means and allow them to make their own conclusions. You just pass on whatever information you feel is true to you and if it is not true to you, discard it. Do not express it simply because either I, or anyone else, say so. We pass through what we know and of course we do not know everything, but we are, in all sincerity, working for the Masters and we hope to help others in that same pursuit.

Now I will leave it there for this week. Thank you for coming and I hope you do not feel that you have wasted time. We realise our friend here is not well and we must not tax her too much today, but she did need your company today to help lift her. She needed your energies and ours and we will try to give it to her.[1]

---

[1] I had bronchitis. The Spirits are always careful if I am not well!

TWENTY THREE

Christmas Discussion

Well, I could almost wish you all a happy Christmas, couldn't I? On this subject I do not become involved in controversial discussion about whether there actually was a Christ or not, so we will go into the deeper meaning of Christmas if you like. I think most of you will probably be aware, and agree with me, that when we think of the Christ energy, it is as that spark of God within each of us, so that each of us is a son or a daughter of God, or a light of God. You are each a sun of God and in fact Christmas should be celebrated each day, not just once a year. Of course the story has been perpetuated and it is a good way to introduce children to it, perhaps as a family, but it has become limited to some extent by happening just one time of the year. It is also symbolic for the Northern hemisphere, in the sense that the physical light is at its lowest and the bulbs and the little plants all die back into the soil and rest, so something goes on in the dark, if you like, within. That spark of God within yourselves is doing a similar sort of thing, and when your Spring comes your shoots will spread forth and your blossom will emerge at the appropriate time; when you have become God conscious. Would anybody like to make a comment on this point? Do you feel that it is acceptable to you?

It comes from the old idea in the Northern hemisphere, doesn't it, which predated the Christian idea, the dying and coming to life again; it is celebrating coming back.

It is a Christ of the Mass, a mass of the people, going into the quiet, into the silence. The Mass in the Catholic Church would involve, would it not, people gathering and sitting quietly?

The man Jesus exemplified the influence of the Christ spirit and therefore the idea, perhaps symbolically, is helpful to a lot of people.

But then it seems to divide people, does it not, because it is so difficult to prove; first that Mary was a virgin and secondly that Jesus was actually the son of God. Because it is in the past and no-one can actually prove it physically, it divides people. But by becoming aware that the Christ is everywhere, if you are sincere and you follow the path, you can in fact prove it to yourselves. It's difficult when you have to accept hearsay all the time without anybody being able to say, 'Well, I have experienced this', but there are many beings now, are there not, who are able to experience this awareness of God. They are also beginning to feel some element of Godliness within them, and by following certain guidelines you could prove it to yourselves, step by step. Obviously one has to have a certain amount of trust in some form of teaching. So you need to learn to trust your teachers, whoever you choose, and you take one step at a time. If that gives you confidence in your teacher, or in yourself, that you are following the right path, this is helpful. But if you just think rather vaguely what happened to someone else many, many years ago, it can in fact allow people to feel that they no longer have to do anything; that they can just hand everything over because they believe, and that this is sufficient. It would eventually get them there but it will take that much longer because it is not part of personal responsibility.

Our problem is perhaps with the name, the Christ, which of course would only be accepted in certain civilisations.

It's true. That is why there are different teachers living in different bodies in different parts of the world, to give the kind of teaching that is worded in a way that is acceptable. But of course things are beginning to spread and intermingle more and perhaps people with intelligence are coming to realise, despite the different wording, that all are actually learning about the same thing. This spread of books and reading, the more it introduces people to books and to the joy of reading, the more they can search out for themselves. I know there are many kinds of teaching surfacing but they are all part of the pathway up the mountain, some take a little longer than others but there is a path for everyone, whatever suits the different personality, and to which they are drawn.

Do you think sometimes they are drawn to paths that one strays up, and turns round and comes back again?

Oh yes, there are a few of those as well and one gets sidetracked. One can start off with all good intent but of course there are the temptations on the way, too, and one can meander off your pathway quite a bit.

Is it a bit like a game of snakes and ladders?

It is rather like that; yes, a good analogy.

There are many religions on this earth which have in fact divided man. Personally, I pray to God. I don't attempt to impose him on others, and it does seem tragic that a religion has in fact separated different groups of people as we've seen in Yugoslavia just recently.

Very divisive.

Is there any answer to this, or is it just done to increase their knowledge so that man eventually understands?

Yes, it is the problem of the ones who are still at the stage where, because they think they know everything, they impose it on others around them, instead of allowing freedom of choice. It is only as the soul advances in knowledge that it becomes more aware of allowing other souls the freedom of choice. It is usually a very young soul who tries to impose what it believes on to others. It's very similar to civilisations that evolve, become fuller in wisdom, but then along comes a younger civilisation that is still at the fighting stage which takes over the older ones by force. I rather feel myself that this is the way that the older civilisations come to the end of their karma and pass into the next dimensions. It is not seen as very fortunate for those left behind but usually those left behind are those who have not persisted in following their spiritual teachings, so they have had to cope with what has been left behind. Do you understand this?

We've been given a very interesting document said to have come from space people through a channel. It says that they have a religion, but they regard our religions as irreligious because they divide instead of uniting us. Their belief is that there is one supreme, ineffable power beyond our ability to comprehend. They give it the name of God if they communicate with us, because we're used to it, and this power is in every living soul and everything, and it is gradually evolving.

That is the teaching of the highest nature.

Have you any information about other civilisations in space of which we have no knowledge?

There is a great deal of information but it is not my purpose to talk of it at this present moment. We could perhaps go into that at some other date. It is one of those things that it is not easy to prove. There are many sightings and many people have their beliefs as to whether they exist or not, and whatever I say people will continue to believe in exactly the same way afterwards. So we will not go into that just at the moment. It is good to think about.

Some people complain of the commercialisation of Christmas, but in his poem John Betjeman said that all the ties and scarves and coloured shirts that are given away are symbols of love; we should not be too hard on it.

There are many levels of love. There are those that are given in the purest sense and there are others that are struggling with their desire for self and their desire to impress. So there are varying degrees. For those that do not give with love it is a good exercise. At least they have been brought into the idea of giving, even if it has a selfish motive to start with, but people would benefit more if they could celebrate more of the silence and less of the heartiness. It is not because I wish to be a party pooper – I have enjoyed my parties in the past – but it is because much of the Christmas spirit has been lost and there is so much worry about how to pay for all these presents and this puts rather a damper on the celebrations, does it not? And the work invariably falls upon the woman of the house, or even the man if he is being the 'mother.' It is basically the children for whom people would like to make something special. But much of this imposed jollity has a great deal of sadness behind it, and the alcohol is consumed to try to overcome the sadness within, so that they can pretend for a little longer.

It is said there are more break-ups and divorces caused over the Christmas period than almost any other, except for holidays!

It is a great exercise in human relationships.

Perhaps it's a good thing for that then.

It is, yes. People come together who would not normally be together and they have to learn to get on, to try to put the needs of others to the forefront of their minds.

So do you think that it's a good idea even then to pursue some of the traditional things coming up to Christmas; a few carols or something for the sake of community? We're holding a 'Peace ' with a meditation for all the world during it but then intend to have a few carols.

There's no harm in that and if there is enjoyment from this, that is fine.

The thing that interests me is whether people who are devout Buddhists, Hindus, Jews and Christians, Taoists, or whatever – does it matter when they pass over what particular religion or geography is imposed upon them?

Not really, no. As long as their motivation is sincere and they are aware of learning to become less selfish, in other words become aware of the God within, that is the basic principle. Whatever names they use or whatever teachings that they follow is all to do with understanding, becoming aware of each other and of God, it does not really matter.

May we ask how you will celebrate Christmas?

Well, of course, we celebrate it every day. It is a union with the God within and we gather together for different occasions. Sometimes we have teachers from the next dimension and there are many souls gathering together in one particular point and I can see the picture of them streaming altogether towards this great light. It is like a magnet which draws us and we have a sense of knowing that the time is now. We all collect together in this great amphitheatre and as we wait in silence there is a great sense of joy and light, of love, and we can see the emanations of the

Being who comes to speak to us, approaching, and this lifts us temporarily into what it would be like for us in the next dimension. It is wonderful.

We sometimes have a sensation that our heart would seem to expand and almost explode. Is there anything similar in your plane?

Yes, you have described that beautifully, my friend. That was the sensation I was experiencing just as I spoke because whatever we think in our dimension, so things are. Even by my thinking of this, it puts me in touch with that point in time; I say in time because I do not really have another word I can use, but it is timelessness. But of course if we are to meet at the same time then there has to be a point somewhere in the now! I'm afraid that's the nearest I can get to it to describe it.

In a way, although your body can be moving around, doing different things, in your mind you can all connect together by thoughts, can you not? And that is regardless of time, and even those of you who are becoming sensitives can become aware when somebody is thinking of you, and become linked together, and in that dimension of your thought, and not in the time that you have when in the physical body.

If you have a guide attached to someone that's working and they need still to be with the person that they're helping, would they send part of themselves back at that time? They wouldn't leave them during that period, would they? Would they send a part of themselves?

The thing is that when we are working with you, we are still in contact, but it is only our minds that contact you. When you see or feel what looks like our bodies, it is a projected thought-form of our bodies as you used to know us, or as we present them to you now. So that we are not divided from you in one sense and we are always in contact with you, if necessary, by thought. It may seem at times that we are not in contact with you by thought, but it simply means that both you and the guide are getting on with what needs to be done. Should you need assistance it would be known immediately because there would be no time lapse, so to speak, so that we can be at these events but still be in touch with you and in fact it can benefit you by our being at rest because we can channel some of the energies back to you.

Do you have music or any other form of art for this kind of meeting?

Well, we hear the sounds that come with the colours and the lights. It is a form of music that is very difficult to reproduce on the earth plane. Some of us do try and you do occasionally get one composer who can replicate it honestly, and as near as possible, but there are not too many of them. But the sounds and the colours are as one and when you get a group of beings together as well, their light is added to that, and their harmony, their sound, joins in. In a way it is symbolised by your orchestras and your choirs. Some people have more melodious voices here, do they not, than others, but once you reach the higher levels the sounds that you send forth when you are sufficiently spiritualised are melodious.

You say this happens every day?

The large gatherings do not happen at every moment. I do not say whether it is today in your terms because all our moments are in the spirit, the great spirit, but this is where I was having difficulty in explaining this time to you.

We can experience the joy within which is our celebration of the Christ spirit or the God energies, in the present terminology, so you can, if you choose, celebrate Christmas every day. It is only the outward show that changes, because people are celebrating the light, and celebrating love because they see it in the form of a baby, the symbol of a new life, a new light, and those who are conscious can become aware of a love that they did not know they had and be aware of the joy that many young parents feel. They did not know that they could feel so much. It is one of those methods by which one can become aware of the depths of feeling, and the joys within each soul. In a way the other celebrations are really just celebrations of the same thing only with a different outward show.

Sometimes we ask a question which seems personal, so that we can get a general idea of conditions and so that we may answer if somebody asks. Could I ask if you have noticed a change in your own awareness since you've passed over? That you gradually, in some way, increase or enlarge?

I'm very pleased to be able to say yes. There is a sense of expanding from the point when I finished my last incarnation, so the continual gentle growth or expansion, at some point, would draw me away from the earth plane, but I will continue to work around the earth plane until that time comes.

We cannot imagine what it must be like to be always light and with no dark night, and not to be able to see the stars and the moon. Can you see anything like that?

It does not go black but it does go into various soft shades and if you feel in your tuning-in the need for such things you envisage things of the earth. Strange?

I love the dark. Can you see stars?

If I need to see the stars I can see them. I can tune in to whatever scene or experience that I may need.

You know we see the man in the moon on this side; as you know down in Australia you have to incline your head to see it being tipped over. Do you see it from that side? Or this side?

If I choose to I can see both. It is all to do with thought, you see. We are not restricted by the limitations of the physical world. I can see through it if I wish to. I can even visit the entities that live within the vibrations of the moon but you would not see them with your physical eye, you would have to tune into the thought-world.

There are times in recent years where I tend to be very emotional and feel, in fact, reduced to tears. Originally I was told I was a weak person but another man realised it was a question of strength. It's a sensitivity that I have, I feel, and I can't really explain it, but it is disarming when one can virtually be reduced. I can quite often have tears in my eyes when years ago that would never have happened.

As you become aware of the spirit within you and you advance on your spiritual path you do find things happening; there's many a man been disconcerted by this sudden bursting into tears; it is possibly because of being part of the English race. We are not encouraged as men to cry but it is a sensitivity. You're quite right and do not be afraid of it. It will ease off in time. Your sensitivity will not disappear, your sensitivity should increase, but possibly the desire to dissolve into tears, into sobs, will ease off. But never be afraid to let the tears flow.

In developing, one is allowing a feminine principle to balance and that feminine principle brings actual tearfulness.

Yes, men are afraid of their feminine side.

Whereas we have to cope with our masculine side as women. I was invited to Plymouth to a planetarium. Professor Seymour there has actually managed to put his life on the line by saying that there is something in astrology as well as astronomy. He is an astronomer and has written a book which is criticised by the scientific world. He has now written one on psychic phenomena and he is talking about the connections that you can't see; the strings between things. In one of these experiments, he talks about two particles going apart from each other, how they break apart, but they are actually still together; they send messages and react in the same way, and he thinks that maybe twins have the same thing, and this is what's connecting them. He's not looking quite on the spiritual side yet, as he's talking about all these emanations. I wonder if there's anything you would like to add to that?

No, I think that's a very interesting event. Before we started speaking I was watching the streams of light coming to earth; each tiny thread of light was connected to every thought.

In order to become more aware of the God within can we just do it through meditation and asking for our guide's help?

You must not forget you are the light already. The reason, if you cannot see it, is because there's a little extra covering that you have acquired over many lifetimes. But by going into meditation, and asking for help, you are giving yourself the chance to go deeper within and make that contact, because most of the time otherwise you spend looking at outward things. I know that most of the time we're thinking about material things or what we should do in our practical life, so through meditation you get a chance to really learn to be in touch and think about spiritual matters and ask for help.

You were kind enough to tell us that you were aware of changes in consciousness during the time that you passed over; are you aware of any changes in what is now your body?

It feels as though the light part of myself seems to expand, so that instead of it being enclosed on other dimensions, when I choose to, and when I really go within myself, into the light, I'm aware of my consciousness expanding far beyond that which I could do when I originally passed over. You are learning in a sense to do that in the meditating, when

I say you go within; but have you not noticed that when you go inside, instead of the space being smaller, you seem to be in a greater space and when you open your eyes, the room that you find yourself in seems much smaller than when you had your eyes closed?

It can be bright inside too, then dark when you open your eyes.

That's right, yes. May I wish you a happy Christmas?

Every day!

Every day.